THE ESSENTIAL
SEA KAYAKER

THE ESSENTIAL SEA KAYAKER

A Complete Course for the Open-Water Paddler

David Seidman

Illustrations by Andy Singer

Ragged Mountain Press
Camden, Maine

International Marine/
Ragged Mountain Press

A Division of The **McGraw·Hill** Companies

11   13   15   17   18   16   14   12

Library of Congress Cataloging-in-Publication Data

Seidman, David.
    The essential sea kayaker : a complete course for the open-water
paddler / David Seidman : illustrations by Andy Singer.
        p.   cm.
    Includes bibliographical references.
    ISBN 0-07-158009-3
    1. Sea kayaking.   I. Title.
GV788.5.S45   1992
797.1'22—dc20   91-15988
                                                                  CIP

Questions regarding the content of this book should be addressed to:

Ragged Mountain Press
P.O. Box 220
Camden, ME 04843

For every book sold, Ragged Mountain Press will make a contribution
to an environmental cause.

The Essential Sea Kayaker is printed on a 60-pound Renew Opaque,
which contains 50 percent recycled waste paper (preconsumer)
and 10 percent postconsumer waste paper.

Edited by Elise Earl
Composition by TAB Books, Blue Ridge Summit, PA,
and Typeworks, Belfast, ME
Production by Molly Mulhern and Dawn Peterson

To Andy,
for showing me how to keep my head above water;

and Ruth,
who took over on land.

On Seamanship

thoughts for those who go to sea in small craft

One of the paradoxes of sea kayaking is the ease with which one can acquire the physical skills required. In just two or three days a person of average balance and dexterity, and with a good coach, can master a relatively advanced level of skills, including kayaking turns, braces and a roll. But as with any form of boating on the sea, this is only the beginning. Because the kayak has an average speed of barely three knots, it is particularly susceptible to the vagaries of currents and wind. Although its shallow draft and light weight mean it can negotiate surf beaches and rocky shores not attempted by other craft, these characteristics render it vulnerable to wind and strong current. It is important that, once the physical skills have been acquired, the many lessons of kayak seamanship begin.

As is true of every way of going on the sea, in big ships or in small kayaks, the disciplines of seamanship—the judgment, the knowledge of the vessel and all its parts, the weather sensibility, and the prudent awareness of one's own skills and strengths—usually take years of learning and constant reinforcement. Sound judgment, as is so often the case with such things, is usually more obvious by its absence than its presence. It is also a beast whose image fades with familiarity and changing circumstance. Fatigue will diminish it and conflicting desires and requirements become the medium for its expression—or lack thereof.

As a beginner, or one of long experience, it is very easy then to miss the whole point, the key ingredient that holds the whole mass together; lose your humility for the sea and the whole thing falls apart.

Go with respect, and live to enjoy.

—John Dowd
Kayak voyager

Contents

Introduction

There was a thick haze this morning and the swells were long, slow, and easy. Still asleep for my first few strokes, a dunking in the cool surf brought me up sharp. I paddled hard then, flying over the inshore waves, which steepened only to collapse behind me. As the bottom dropped away the waves no longer responded to its drag and met me now as gentle rollers. I felt like a bird on the water, gently bobbing in response to the swell. Light, effortless, and perfectly at home. After a short spurt I turned back toward the shore. It was gone in the mist, the only evidence a dull sound of the surf. It could have been any shore on any ocean in the world. And there I was in a very small boat, alone at sea, and it felt wonderful.

A Promise

Like you, I am still learning about sea kayaking. What makes us different is that you now have this book to get you started and help refine the techniques that will make sea kayaking the rewarding and enjoyable sport it should be.

One of the biggest problems with getting started in sea kayaking is that there are very few instructors. Of course the guy who sells you your boat will probably run through the basics; and there's always someone you've met or someone from a local club who will help out. But most of us wind up teaching ourselves and, very likely, making things up as we go along.

That's how I began. I had to make a lot of false starts and spend a lot of time paddling in circles before realizing my mistakes. Fortunately the basics, getting in and paddling around, are easy to grasp in some rudimentary way. The unfortunate part is that techniques learned incorrectly stay with you, and show up as weaknesses, usually at the worst possible times. Even so, I did manage to learn something from those first flounderings, but it could have been a lot easier. And it will be for you.

This book will give you the essence of the sport, the techniques, and the specifics in detail. With that you'll be able to start thinking about long cruises in the Bahamas or getting better aerobic exercise out of an evening's paddle. Sound like what you're looking for? Good, because in the following pages you'll find a place to start and a place to return to as you continue to develop. It'll be easy. I promise.

Know Your Author

Back when I was first starting out I felt that there was a need for a good, basic book on sea kayaking. And since no expert had come up with anything that worked, I decided to go out and find my own expert, learn from him, and then tell you about it in a way that would make sense. The words in this book are mine, speaking as the consummate klutz to you . . . who I hope is much less of one. The substance has been supplied by Andy Singer.

Andy was a rare find, yet in some ways typical of the people involved in sea kayaking. He owns a company whose purported business is to design, build, and sell kayaks. Does he sell many? Not really. He's too busy paddling. He also should charge more for the lessons he gives. But if he feels you aren't getting it, there's no cost; plus, he'll help you find another way to learn. Andy will never be a success, yet couldn't be more of one. He loves what he is doing, and loves sharing it with others.

Andy's been paddling for more than thirty years and teaching for the last ten. He's patient, inventive, and fun to learn from. Whatever I've learned I've gotten from him, which must mean something because I'm still here to write about it.

For the rest of this book you will be Andy's student, too. Since you can't really be there with him, I will be there for you. I'll make the goofs, ask the dumb questions, and then explain it to you. All you'll have to do is read, think, and practice.

What You Are Getting Yourself Into

The term sea kayaking might be a bit misleading. It is rarely done on the open sea; most folks preferring to just putter along the coastlines of bays, lakes, and creeks, watching the scenery. And, while the boats we use are obviously kayaks, they seem more like rugged seagoing craft than the diminutive white water boats we most often associate with the term "kayak." But sea kayaking has a romantic ring to it, so let's leave it as it is.

The sea kayaks we paddle are the product of more than five thousand years of evolution. Coastal people of the Arctic built these craft to deal with the unique problems of their environment, and groups separated by thousands of miles produced what was essentially the same answer. A good indication that what they came up with was sound.

The traditional Arctic kayak was unusually fast and safe. Its closed deck and sealed cockpit made it watertight and virtually unsinkable. Its low profile reduced its susceptibility to wind and waves. The novel double paddle made it responsive and easy to balance under the most extreme conditions. When capsized it could be rolled upright with a minimum of effort, making it, in effect, as self-righting as a lifeboat. The end result was one of the safest deepwater vessels ever created, and it supported large cultures for thousands of years. This is the legacy of today's sea kayak.

Is Sea Kayaking for You?

The demographics show the average sea kayaker to be in his or her thirties, college educated, financially secure, and as likely to be a woman as a man. But these are only numbers on a chart. By nature sea kayakers seem more contemplative than white water kayakers, appreciating the simple act of paddling and exhilarating in the subtle rather than the immediate and obvious. They also seem to possess a natural affinity for the smell, feel, and moods of open water, and are often just as comfortable in the water as on it. If this sounds like you, you may be one of us.

Don't let age stop you. Eskimos encouraged their children to play in kayaks from about five years on, and by twelve they were learning to roll upright from an inverted position. Kids around eight or nine years of age have a remarkable sense of balance and movement, and do surprisingly well as compared with adult novices. Seniors should not be scared off either. The kayak's seated position is comfortable and supportive, and the exercise of paddling can be as strenuous or leisurely as one likes, perfect for low-impact upper body and aerobic exercise.

I would also like to encourage the disabled to try sea kayaking. For most of the physically challenged there is very little here that cannot be overcome with a little ingenuity. If you have use of your hands, arms, torso, and can swim, you'll find that once in the kayak you become as fluid and mobile as the next person, with an equal chance of finding adventure or discovering quiet pleasures.

How to Use This Book

I've laid things out in a progressive format. You start here, go there next, and then finally wind up where you want to be. Once you've learned something, you'll use it to learn something else. As ideas accumulate you'll be surprised how far you've progressed.

In part, this book was written because there is a severe shortage of instructors. Although you can teach yourself almost everything you might need to know, do not give up looking for a good teacher. If he or she makes things seem difficult, if you are making very little progress, or he or she can't isolate your problems, find someone else. But keep on with the book while you're searching.

Remember that this or any other book on sea kayaking is worthless unless you get out there on the water and try what you've been reading about. Read, yes. Study, yes. Listen to other paddlers, sure. But your time on the water and the mistakes you make will give you the best education.

And forget about equipment. I know for some of you this will be impossible. There are always those who love the paraphernalia more than the sport or get hopelessly mired in technicalities. Thankfully, though, there isn't much in the way of gear that you'll need or can even buy. And the technicalities were worked out a few thousand years ago by people whose lives, not quality time, depended on it.

So get out there, get wet, have fun, and do it!

David Seidman

Sea Kayaking 101:

SETTING FORTH

The first part of this course, SK 101, is not just for beginners. While it is a place to start, it is also a place to come back to. If you are just beginning, it is here that you'll develop traits that will stand you in good stead for the rest of your paddling days. If you have sea time already, this section will be a good way to check your technique and refine what you already know.

It has been said that the person claiming ten years' experience is likely to be someone with one year of learning and nine years of repeating the same things. So don't feel proud about coming back to make sure you've gotten the fundamentals down pat.

In SK 101 you'll gather the equipment you'll need, get used to it, get moving, and sample things to come.

If you're new to sea kayaking, follow the sections in the order presented. The book has been designed to build upon experience. Read one complete section and then stop. Get a good overview of the principles behind it. Then go out and tackle that section one step at a time. Work on it until you feel comfortable with what you are doing. If in doubt, and you can't find an experienced guide, have someone else read and go over the step that troubles you. Even though the reader might not understand sea kayaking, he or she will at least bring an objective point of view to the problem.

There are no great mysteries to the basic techniques of sea kayaking. Just keep trying

and eventually you'll get them. But you're going to have to work at it in the beginning, so don't get bogged down if things don't flow at first.

Don't pressure yourself either. Sea kayaking is not a competitive pastime. Someday your only challenger will be the open water and it couldn't care less. But for now, in the beginning, it's only your ego. So back off, go easy on yourself, and enjoy the learning. If you feel that you're not getting the hang of one step, go on to the others in that section. Work around it, while periodically coming back to it. Eventually, and not too far in the future, it will all come together.

There are paddlers out there who taught themselves. If you are one of these people, you might look through SK 101 and think that it's not for you. But it is. Even though you might be able to perform all of the maneuvers, there is more often than not one small but key ingredient you've missed: something that will make your life easier, your paddling less strenuous, or your trips a little safer. As with many of us, you might be substituting strength and luck for the ultimate reliability of a perfected style.

Remember: Overconfidence, and the false sense of security that comes with it, has created more frightening situations for sea kayakers than anything else. The only way to know your limits is to know yourself. And the only way to know yourself is to gauge your ability against a set of standards. This book will provide those standards.

WHAT YOU WILL NEED

The Kayak

First we should come to an agreement on what a sea kayak is. You could, of course, go to sea in almost any kind of kayak, but a more realistic approach would be to have a boat that maximizes your safety, comfort, efficiency, and enjoyment.

Since it will spend most of its time on a straight course rather than twisting around rocks in a river, a sea kayak needs to be directionally stable. That is, it should not force the paddler to work at keeping it going in a straight line. Since the sea kayak depends on the paddler for all of its forward momentum, it should require only a minimum of effort to achieve and maintain a fast cruising speed. Since you will probably spend long periods in the kayak, it must offer an acceptable level of creature comfort. It should also provide another type of comfort that relates to handling the waters it is sent out to meet. This comfort is known as seaworthiness and is the ultimate test of the sea kayak's abilities.

As you can see, the boat described is job-specific. It will be good for one thing and that one only. It would be hopelessly awkward on narrow rivers and almost useless in white water. But if your goal is to venture onto open waters, put many miles under your keel, or poke your bow around the next headland, then the boat defined as a sea kayak is right for you.

Now that we have a generic definition, we can explore the more specific aspects of your personal sea kayak. For it is here that we can start narrowing the field to help you find the boat that will best fit your needs.

It is here that beginners may go a little crazy. And rightfully so. How do you pick the proper kayak when you have no basis for your choice? The answer is you don't. And that's OK.

If you listen to every expert you'll never come to a decision. Your best option is to get as close as you can to a general-purpose touring sea kayak (15 to 17 feet long, by 23 to 25 inches wide, and of moderate carrying capacity) with a good resale value. Starting with a middle-of-the-road design and the philosophy that your first boat isn't going to have to last you the rest of your life will make things a lot easier.

Don't be afraid to go by your instincts. As much as you can with anything new, make sure that your first boat feels right, not awkward or threatening. Try as many boats as you can in the water, then buy the one you feel the most relaxed in and is most appealing to your eye. (Kayaking is personal stuff, and looks definitely count!) If it feels and looks right, you'll use it. And the more you use it, the faster you'll learn. As you gain experience your ideas about the right boat will change, sometimes dramatically. Every chance you get, rent, beg, or borrow other kayaks.

A good place to start may be with any of the polyethylene plastic kayaks made by the larger manufacturers. There is nothing extreme in their designs, they have all the basic features, are almost indestructible, paddle reasonably well, and maintain a good resale value. They are also comparatively inexpensive. So if you find that sea kayaking is not for you, you haven't made a large investment in something that is going to wind up as a planter in your backyard.

If these boats don't appeal to you, consider any of the fiberglass kayaks that may be popular in your area. Again, think moderate design and good resale. By all means get a boat you like and are proud of, but be willing to start modestly, saving your dollars and experience for the next one.

Once you do have a realistic understanding of your requirements, the act of choosing a kayak becomes the single most important step in directing your involvement in the sport. The boat you pick will affect your choice of paddle, paddling style, accessories, and psychological attitude. Sound intimidating? Well, don't worry. Remember: No one has yet found the perfect kayak. And if anyone did, he would probably try to improve it somehow.

The first question in choosing a kayak is: "How do you envision yourself using it?"

If the idea of long expeditions into the wilderness attracts you, you'll want something with a lot of space for stowage. This will probably necessitate a broad beam with an associated increase in stability, which might also appeal to you. It will have to be rugged and therefore is likely to be heavy. A boat that

WHAT YOU WILL NEED

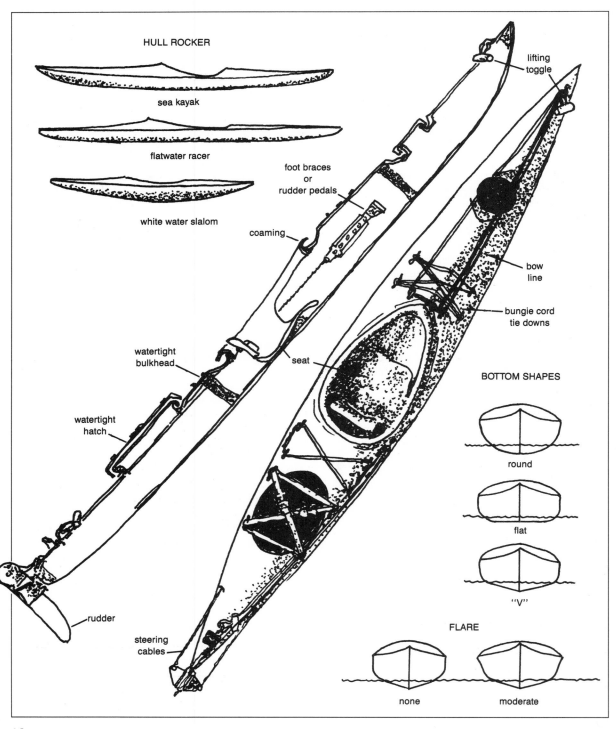

HULL ROCKER

sea kayak

flatwater racer

white water slalom

lifting toggle

foot braces or rudder pedals

coaming

bow line

bungie cord tie downs

watertight bulkhead

seat

watertight hatch

BOTTOM SHAPES

round

flat

"V"

FLARE

moderate

rudder

steering cables

comes apart for easier shipping could also be handy.

For nature watching or fishing you'll want a very stable kayak that can be left to its own devices while you deal with equipment or fish. It would also be advantageous to have a boat that could turn quickly or within a limited space.

If you're just interested in short day trips, and almost 40 percent of all sea kayakers are, you'll want a boat that can reach its best speed with a minimum of effort. It should be something lively and fast that will give you an invigorating workout, and challenge your abilities.

Once you've decided how you will use the boat, you have to start thinking about which type of kayak will do the best job. Ask yourself what trade-offs you are willing to make to satisfy your goals. Here are some choices and the compromises that go with them.

Single or Double?

If you will always be paddling with someone else then it is worth considering a double, a kayak for two paddlers. Doubles are ideal if you and your partner are of significantly different strengths or abilities. Doubles also cost about a third less than two singles, are theoretically faster because of their longer length, more stable, and often more comfortable in rough seas. On the other hand, a double is not as responsive as a single, it has less stowage than two singles, it offers less personal freedom, and it cannot be easily paddled by one person.

Slow and Stable, or Fast and Tippy?

Here are a few guidelines regarding performance.

Wide boats are generally slower and more stable than narrow ones. Narrow boats require less force to move them than wide boats. The longer the waterline length, the higher a boat's potential top speed.

Flat-bottomed boats are steady when upright, with stability increasing rapidly to a specific angle of heel, after which they can capsize abruptly. "V"-bottomed boats are less steady in the upright position, with stability increasing as they are heeled over and the capsizing point gradually reached. Round-

bottomed boats are the least steady of all, being just as stable upright as when tilted. It is also the form of least resistance, presenting the minimum of wetted surface area for a given volume. Adding flare to the sides of any of these hull forms increases their stability at extreme angles. Most sea kayaks have gently rounded hulls that incorporate a little of each bottom type and flare.

Speed and maneuverability are incompatible. The more curve (rocker) in a boat's bottom as seen in profile, the slower the boat, but the easier it will be to turn. For example, the flat-water racer, which has almost no rocker, can be moved through the water with minimal effort but is extremely difficult to turn. The exact opposite is true of the highly-rockered white water slalom kayak, with the touring sea kayak being somewhere in between.

Real-world speed differences between kayaks are not all that great. Most can be easily paddled at 3 knots, with short spurts to 4 or 5. A boat might have a 6-knot potential, but few recreational paddlers could get it there. More important than ultimate speed is the ease with which you can move the boat.

For those who are more athletic and adventuresome a swift yet tippy boat will be best. You can go farther and faster for a given energy output, but you pay in reduced stability.

For those who are more conservative, a stable boat will be best. You will have to work harder to keep it going, but to some degree it will look after itself when you can't, and it will place fewer demands on your capabilities as a paddler.

There are boats that compromise and try to give you a little of each—or none of either, depending on how you look at it.

Rigid or Collapsible?

The only reason not to purchase a rigid boat is if you intend to take it with you on an airplane or your only storage facility is a closet.

Collapsible boats can either be take-apart or folding. Take-apart kayaks are usually standard fiberglass models that have been sectionalized. They do not store as compactly, are more expensive, and are more vulnerable to damage in shipping than folding ones, but their carrying capacity and performance is usually superior.

Folding boats stretch a canvas-like skin over an assembled wood or aluminum frame and can be stowed in one to three bags. They tend to be wider, slower, quieter, and more stable than rigid kayaks. They have also proven to be extremely seaworthy, but lacking in the performance and efficiency of a rigid kayak. They are more expensive and require considerably more care in their use and upkeep. While assembly averages only 20 minutes and disassembly a little longer, this could become a tedious chore if done on a regular basis.

For rigid construction, probably the best material to date is fiberglass. It can be made strong, flexible, and light, with the average single kayak weighing 55 pounds. Kevlar can be incorporated into fiberglass construction to reduce weight, while simultaneously retaining strength and increasing cost.

Roto-molded, polyethylene plastic construction is stronger and 25 percent less expensive, but about 10 percent heavier, than fiberglass. Plastic is placed in a sealed, heated mold that is rotated. When the melted plastic cools, you have a one-piece kayak. These boats are almost indestructible but can be deformed by heat or uneven pressure if improperly stored or transported.

Meeting Your Standards

Once you have narrowed your choice to a type of sea kayak, you have to judge if the specific boat you've chosen meets your standards.

- Are you and your boat a good fit? All kayaks require internal adjustments but the fit should at least be close. Take into consideration if there is enough foot room and support or contact points for your knees, thighs, hips, rear, and lower back. Sit in it for a while before passing judgment. Never buy a boat without trying it on.

- Is there enough stability to make you feel secure? Does its stability feel predictable, or does it become suddenly unstable if leaned too far?

- Is it easy to paddle? A good way to judge

this is by paddling into a headwind and waves.

- How difficult is it to turn or to paddle in a straight line? How does it want to point in relation to the wind when still and when underway?

- Do you like its looks? Since you will be spending a lot of time with it you might as well. Color is important, too. Yellow is the most visible, white shows the least wear, and deep blues and red fade the fastest.

- Is it too heavy for you to lift and carry by yourself? Would it be too difficult to hoist on a car rack?

- Is there enough reserve buoyancy in the form of airbags or watertight bulkheads to float you and the boat when it is swamped?

- Are there fittings such as lifting toggles, bow line for being towed, deck bungie cords, and good watertight hatches? Are they strong and up to the job?

- Does it need and have a skeg or rudder?

- Can it hold all your gear without your having to lash any on deck?

- Is it well built? Only a professional can really judge this but there are clues. Check the finish both inside and out. See how things fit, especially in hidden areas. If the builder cared about the details he probably brought a similar attitude to the rest of the construction.

- Price? An expensive boat is not always a good boat; but an inexpensive one rarely is. Remember that quality costs initially but pays off in the long run.

The Paddle

The double-bladed paddle is used to propel, alter direction, and provide a stabilizing force. It works as part of an integrated system that also includes the kayak and your body. All three components interlock and affect each other in a way that is infinitely variable. This is why choosing the right paddle is so important, yet at the same time so difficult and subjective.

The paddle works as a variable lever which, through the movable fulcrum supplied by your lower hand, digs into the water so you can pull the kayak toward and past it. Through careful choices you can make sure that this lever matches your capabilities so as not to put undue strain on joints and muscles, while still providing the necessary thrust for the hull you are attached to. Balance is the key.

Materials

You can immediately put this balance in your favor by using the lightest paddle possible. Naturally you won't want to forfeit strength to do this. To get both strength and lightness takes money, but it will be money well spent, and the investment will look better with each hour you spend holding the paddle. Average paddles weigh 2 1/2 pounds. Over three pounds is too heavy and under two is the domain of costly, high-tech materials.

A well-made, laminated wood paddle is still the desirable standard. Without a doubt the worst is an aluminum shaft with plastic blades. It will be cold to the touch, heavy, poorly balanced, and usually ill-formed, but it will be cheap. The best for general service is fiberglass for both shaft and blade. It is strong, light, has some spring to it, and feels warm to the touch. Exotic cores or reinforcements (such as carbon fibers, graphite, or Kevlar) can be incorporated into a fiberglass paddle to reduce weight without sacrificing strength. . . for a price.

Length

The next step is to ascertain the proper paddle length and blade type for your personal style, which is a combination of the pace (cadence) and force with which you feel most comfortable under most circumstances.

Your boat, and how you sit in it, will be the first factor. If your seated position is low in the kayak, or if the kayak is wide, you will need a long paddle to reach the water. A second influencing factor will be how easily your boat moves through the water. Sluggish boats match up better with long paddles, while less resistant boats do best with shorter ones.

The third factor is your preference for a particular cadence. All other things being equal, longer paddles require a slower stroke with a lot more power behind them than shorter paddles. The energy output will be the same for both, but only one (or something in between) will feel comfortable for you and your particular kayak. Try a variety of paddles from 7 to 8 1/2 feet long, all with the same blade shape. Paddle into a moderate headwind for about 15 minutes with each. You'll know right off which feels most comfortable.

The Blade

Blades too will influence your style of paddling. Blades with a lot of area or a shape that grips the water (such as a curved blade), require a lot of power behind them. Blades with less area, or a slippery shape (such as a narrow blade), require less power.

Don't be fooled by blades that seem to slip. They are not wasting energy. They may be slower to accelerate a boat, but they will keep it going at a constant rate with a lot less effort and impact on your body. By comparison, blades that seem to dig in will accelerate a boat faster, which will help in making turns or using the paddle to provide an upward force to enhance stability. Both work when used for the job they are intended for.

For example, the traditional long and narrow Eskimo blade was dictated by the fact that the user had to paddle great distances at a steady speed over open water. Bursts of power were rare. At the other extreme is the modern paddler in white water or surf, who needs a wide blade with its more immediate grip on the water for sudden applications of power to move, steer, or right himself. Both are working as efficient levers.

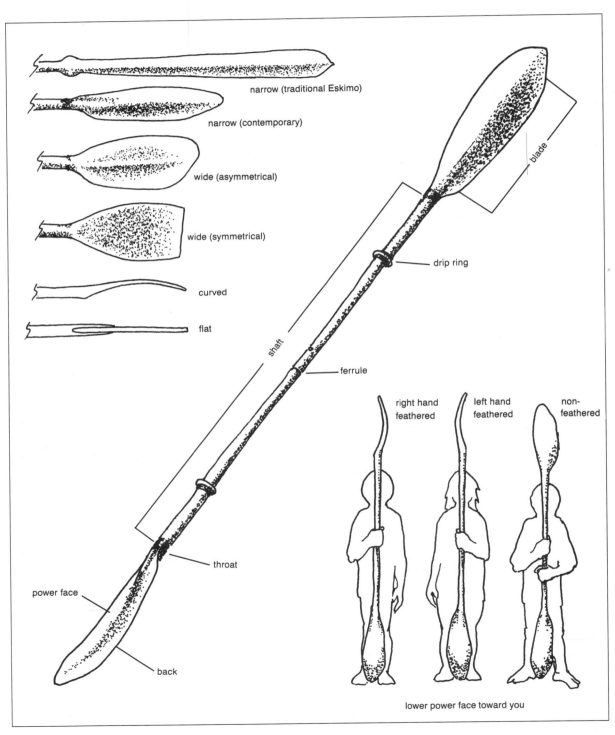

narrow (traditional Eskimo)

narrow (contemporary)

wide (asymmetrical)

wide (symmetrical)

curved

flat

blade

drip ring

shaft

ferrule

right hand feathered

left hand feathered

non-feathered

throat

power face

back

lower power face toward you

To select the best blade for you and your boat, test paddles of the same length but different blade types by paddling into the wind for at least 15 minutes with each. Also try bracing strokes to find which blades give you an acceptable amount of support.

A blade that is asymmetrical—that is, one with unequal areas on each side of the centerline running the length of the blade—is a definite asset. This balances the load on the blade to reduce twisting forces and improves efficiency. Blade tips that are angled rather than straight across have the same effect.

No one paddle length, blade type, or combination thereof will be right for all conditions. Wind strength, sea state, your experience, and your varying levels of energy will all be factors. Intelligent compromise is the best we can hope for. This may seem a daunting and somewhat cavalier proposal. Find a comfortable paddle length as described above, using a blade that is either flat or only mildly curved. This type of blade will often be less expensive, and is easier to orient with respect to the water in different movements.

Feathered or Non-feathered

When selecting a paddle you will also have to decide whether it is to be feathered or non-feathered. A feathered paddle has its blades offset 70 to 90 degrees from each other; the paddle is designated as either right- or left-hand controlled, depending on how the blades' power (concave) faces are oriented. A non-feathered paddle has both blades on the same plane. Rather than buying three paddles to find which style you like best, buy one take-apart paddle that can be set to all three positions. This will let you experiment and give you a good on-board spare paddle once you have decided which way you want to go. When purchasing a take-apart paddle, inspect the connecting joint, known as the ferrule, for strength and a minimum amount of play.

Neither feathering nor non-feathering is superior, and both have their advocates and detractors. Feathering is thought to have a slight mechanical advantage and to offer less wind resistance on the airborne blade when you are paddling into the wind. Non-feathering

may reduce stress on wrist muscles and offer less resistance on the airborne blade when you are paddling with the wind on your side. Both techniques will be thoroughly reviewed in the section about paddling.

To determine the configuration of your paddle, stand it in front of you with the lower blade's power face pointing toward you. If the upper blade's power face points to your left, it is a left-hand controlled, feathered paddle; to your right, it is a right-hand controlled feathered paddle; if both blades face the same direction, it is a non-feathered paddle. A feathered paddle with flat blades can be either right- or left-handed, because flat blades have no set power faces.

Remember: The best paddle is the one that feels most comfortable when the wind and waves kick up.

The Shaft

Beyond the basics, there are some niceties to look for in a paddle. A shaft that is oval in cross section where it is held by the controlling hand might be advantageous. This shape more closely resembles the way we grasp objects, therefore giving a better grip. It also is used to keep the blades properly aligned to your hand and the water. This last feature may be restrictive to some paddlers who like to alter blade angle to suit their stroke without twisting their wrists into awkward positions. For them a round shaft is best.

To improve your grip, keep the shaft dry by using drip rings. Grip can also be improved by lightly sanding the shaft where it is held by the controlling hand with #400 sandpaper or steel wool. Fiberglass shafts must be sanded gently in order to avoid raising glass fibers, which can very irritating. An alternative is a section of bicycle inner tube or the tape used on tennis racquet handles placed over the shaft.

WHAT YOU WILL NEED

Gear

Must fit (boat & person)

Spray Skirt

It is ironic that the one item which gives a kayak its ultimate seaworthiness is also the one that most frightens people. A spray skirt is made to seal out water and make a kayak completely waterproof and reliably buoyant, not to trap you. Once you begin to feel more at home in your kayak the act of snapping the spray skirt in place brings a certain sense of security with it. It will keep your legs and lower body dry and warm, and you and the boat safe.

A spray skirt is like a waterproof ballerina's tutu. You step into it and pull it up so the skirt part flares out at your waist. The upper part, called a chimney or tunnel, should come to just under your armpits, but not so high that it chafes or is uncomfortable. The tunnel also provides a waterproof seal.

The best, and most expensive, spray skirts are made from neoprene. When stretched, the skirt makes a taut deck that easily sheds water and the tunnel fits snugly around the torso making a flexible, yet waterproof, closure. Because of its snug fit this type of spray skirt often comes in sizes. One size for the skirt, so it will fit the coaming of your boat; and another size for the tunnel, so it will fit you. A properly fitting skirt should not have to be stretched more than 1/2″ on all sides to make a good seal with the coaming. The tunnel is usually marked for your waist size and should be 85 percent of that measurement when unstretched.

An alternative to the neoprene spray skirt is one made from coated nylon. These are lighter, much less expensive, and cooler in warm weather, but the waterproofing will eventually break down or wear as it rubs against the coaming. Nylon skirts do not create as taut a deck as the neoprene, tending to sag and collect water in puddles. Also, nylon tunnels will not fit as snugly or stay up as easily. For those who like the lightness of nylon but don't want to put up with its drawbacks, there are spray skirts made of neoprene but with a nylon tunnel. If built well, these can be a comfortable and secure compromise.

One of the problems with spray skirts is that they limit access to equipment inside the boat. Zippers used to be a common solution but tended to leak. As an alternative many

spray skirt

skirts are made with an external pouch on the tunnel to hold equipment. Make sure pouches close securely with velcro and can be drained of any accumulated water.

Whatever type you choose make sure it fits. While kayak shop owners are probably the nicest bunch of guys to deal with, they are still businessmen and try to stock as few sizes of spray skirts as possible. Don't be convinced that the one or two they have will necessarily fit your boat. Buy one on the condition that it can be returned if it doesn't work out. Then take it home and try these tests to see if it fits you and the boat.

fitting

Without you in it, put the skirt on the boat and then try to pick up the kayak by the skirt's tunnel. A skirt that is too loose will slip right off, one that is too tight will hold on forever. A good fit will hold the boat for a few seconds and then slowly lose its grip. Another test is to put the spray skirt on, get in the boat, and seal the skirt around the coaming. Now draw your knees up and try to stand. The skirt should resist but eventually come free. A good spray skirt also must not hinder your movements. Leaning all the way forward, back, and to the sides should not cause it to come off. To see how the spray skirt will stand up to a breaking wave, put it on the boat while wet. If the fit is correct, it will not pop off when given a good solid thump at its center. Be particularly wary of polyethylene plastic kayaks. The coamings on these are very slippery and need spray skirts that have special neoprene or rubber strips to help maintain a grip.

The proper way to use a spray skirt is to step into it, pull it up as high as you can, and then roll up the rear hem of the skirt before boarding the boat. Once seated roll down the hem in the back and stretch it over the rear coaming. Next stretch the skirt over the front coaming and then seal the remaining sides. Make sure that the elastic in the hem is pushed all the way under the coaming lip and that the grab loop at the front has not been tucked under the skirt. This is your rip cord for a fast escape and it should be right there when you need it. To release the spray skirt, first pull the grab loop forward and then up. Pulling straight up puts a strain on the stitching and increases wear on the front edge of the skirt. To free the rest of the skirt, run your fingers along the inside of the coaming to release the elastic all the way around. If in an emergency you find that you cannot locate the grab loop, lean to one side, grab the folds that will gather at that side, and pull up.

PFD

A PFD (Personal Flotation Device) is what most of us would call a life jacket. The federal government, through the United States Coast Guard, requires that you carry an approved PFD on board every time you go out. Legally you are only required to have one handy, but

PFD

realistically you should always have one on.

On most vessels a person puts a PFD on only when their boat is about to go out from under them. While it is unlikely that your kayak will sink, it could capsize; then you will need all the buoyancy you can get. Capsizes happen suddenly and trying to get into a PFD in the water, while holding onto the kayak and paddle, is almost impossible. PFDs work for you while you're still in the kayak, too. If you try to prevent a capsize, or do go over and attempt an Eskimo roll, a PFD might give you that extra edge to make it back up. A close-fitting PFD also acts as an insulating layer in the water and in the air. All very good reasons to wear yours every time out.

The Coast Guard offers three categories of PFDs from which to choose. Each Coast Guard approved PFD, and this is the only kind you should consider, is labeled to indicate the type and service it is approved for.

- Type I is designated as an Offshore Life Jacket with a minimum buoyancy of 22 pounds. It is thoroughly appropriate for abandoning ship on the high seas; and since a ratio of one pound of flotation for each ten pounds of body weight is considered ideal, it is obviously more than adequate for most of us. While they may be safe, they are too big, bulky, and restrictive to be worn when paddling a kayak.

- Type II is an economy version of the above, typically found growing mold in the lockers of pleasure boats, and can be bought at any discount marine supply store. It does not have as much buoyancy as the Type I, but is designed to do essentially the same job, only under much less extreme conditions. Since their flotation capability is less, and they are just as clumsy as the Type I, paddlers have avoided this type of PFD, too.

- The Type III was created for sport use and, if designed properly, can be ideal for kayaking. Since they are meant to support an active paddler, and not an unconscious castaway, the Coast Guard prefers manufacturers to call them "Flotation Aids" and not "Life Jackets." Either way they guarantee a minimum of 15½ pounds of flotation, and some have more, which is plenty for our purposes. The deciding factor in choosing a Type III is its fit.

When shopping remember that a PFD is always the outermost garment and will be worn over a variety of clothing. Make sure that there is enough adjustability to go over a sweater and paddling jacket, a wetsuit, or only a tee shirt. It should be a snug fit but not to the extent that it restricts any head, body, or arm motions. You may find that the ones made of narrow, vertical foam panels are less rigid than the ones that are solid slabs. Those that provide flotation all the way around the body, including the sides, are better insulators. They are also the ones most likely to restrict arm motions. Try a few windmills and thrash about with your arms, if you make frequent contact in the store it will probably mean chafing on the water.

PFD length will be limited by your spray skirt. One that is too long will be forced up around your ears. The "shorty" type that comes down to your last rib is the right length for kayak use, but may be bulky. Another type has lower panels that roll up and flare out on top of the skirt. These are less bulky but can form a semirigid structure that prevents easy movement, especially toward the back.

Check for adequate fasteners such as belts and ties to keep the PFD from riding up around you while in the water. You can test this on land by putting your arms over your head and having someone push up on the bottom. Ties should be of a quick-release type that can be worked with cold, wet fingers.

If you want your PFD to last do not sit or put heavy weights, such as the kayak, on it. Each time the foam is compressed, buoyancy is reduced. Heat and sunlight also degrade flotation. A natural attrition of three percent per year means that every few years you should consider getting a new PFD. If you are floating with your nose underwater, it's probably time to buy another.

Thinking about improving your PFD? Be careful. Almost anything you do to it will void its Coast Guard approval. What you can do is tie a whistle to the zipper pull, cut belts to length, or put on reflective adhesive tape. What you cannot do is stitch anything to the PFD. If your

PFD has a pocket without a drain hole, put one in. This will not affect the PFD's performance except for the better, although it will probably void the approval. But don't worry, I'll never tell them you did it.

Audible Signal

The government also thinks you should carry "any device capable of making an efficient sound signal audible for 1/2 nautical mile." The main purpose of this is to warn whomever you happen to be sharing the water with that you are there. Being so low in the water sea kayaks have a way of becoming invisible to operators of sail and motor boats. A secondary use is for communication between kayaks traveling together.

You could conceivably get away with a whistle, and there are some available that technically meet Coast Guard requirements, but their range is limited. If purchasing a policeman's type of whistle, make sure that the "pea" will not disintegrate in water.

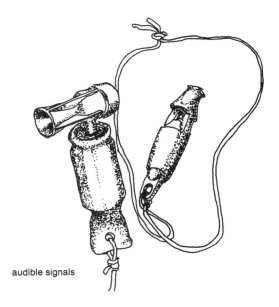

audible signals

For a few dollars more you can get a small freon-charged horn from a bicycle or marine supply store. They have a range of up to one mile, weigh only a few ounces, fit in the palm of your hand, and give about 100 blasts per

replaceable cartridge (keep a spare on board). They are best stowed in an accessible garment pocket or on deck so as to be immediately available when needed.

Putting things under the bungie cords on deck is handy, but far from secure. The solution for your mini horn is to slide the freon canister into a section of bicycle tube leaving a little tube left over. Then punch a hole in the excess through which you can lead a short piece of line. Tie the line to something secure and trap the horn under the bungies. The line will keep it from being washed overboard and the rubber tube will keep the canister from scratching the deck.

Bailers

Kayaks are supposed to be watertight boats; this is what assures their ultimate safety. But nothing with openings can be made absolutely waterproof, so from time to time you'll be sharing your kayak with varying amounts of water.

Typically the most you will have to deal with is a small drip from leaky fittings, hatches, or spray skirts. For this there is nothing better than a sponge. Both aesthetically and pragmatically the best sponge you can get is a large natural one. They are more absorbent, tougher, and soft to the touch. Next best is your basic synthetic bilge sponge from a marine supply store. Make it the biggest and roundest you can find. All sponges have a way of getting lost, especially if the boat happens to fill with water. Make sure to secure the sponge with a short length of line passed through it to the boat.

When your kayak does fill with water you'll want to empty it as quickly as possible, and very often you will be doing this while swimming alongside. The easiest, and cheapest, way to bail is with a plastic container that has its bottom cut off. Get one that is round, as rigid as possible, has a good size handle, and a cap that screws on and will not rust. Fishermen have been using old Clorox bottles for decades; take a clue from them. Like the sponge, make sure your bailer is secured to the boat.

You can also use the plastic bailer while in the boat, but this entails pulling back the spray

skirt, inviting even more water in on a rough day. To empty the kayak with the skirt on you have three options: an electric, deck-mounted, or hand-held pump.

For those who love gadgets and don't mind spending money there are small, self-contained electric bilge pumps specially made for kayaks. They are easy to use and the larger ones move a good stream of water; but they bring their own problems with additional weight, installation, and maintenance.

bailers

Many British kayaks come with a diaphragm pump mounted on their after decks, and there is no reason why you can't add one to your boat. The advantages of these are that the pump is always there when you want it, requires only one hand to operate, and is almost impossible to clog. The disadvantages are that they usually displace very small amounts of water for the effort put in, and you may have to hold the intake hose with your other hand to reach the water.

The cheapest and most common method of pumping is with a hand-held model. To use, you simply stick it down the front of the spray skirt's tunnel and pump away. Typically these are 18″ plastic bilge pumps which are tough, light in weight, and, depending on the model, can move from 6 to 10 gallons per minute. You'll find a variety of pump lengths. But remember that while the longer pumps hold and move more water, they are often awkward to use. The problem with hand-held pumps is that they require two hands, one to hold the pump and the other to do the work. Another problem is that these pumps sink when full of water. To avoid this attach a ring of foam, (such as used to insulate pipes) and secure it to the pump with glue or tape. Now that it won't sink you have to keep it from floating away.

To prevent this, many paddlers keep their pumps in the kayak stuck between the seat support and the side of the boat; this is a good safe place. Do not stow it under the bungie cord on deck since it might come free in a capsize. Wherever you stow it make sure it is accessible yet secure.

figure eight
loop knot

Bow Line

There are times when you will need to tie up your kayak while on land or be towed by another vessel while at sea. For both instances do not expect someone else to supply the line. Bring your own and keep it rigged and ready.

A permanent installation can be made by tying one end of 1/4-inch (minimum) braided nylon or Dacron line to a secure fitting on the bow of your kayak. This can be the fitting through which the grab loop is run or the grab loop itself. Attach the line using a figure eight loop knot, leaving a large enough loop that more line can be passed through. Lead the free end of the line back to a fitting, (such as an eye strap used to hold down the bungies) near but to one side of the cockpit. Pass the line through this fitting, back up to the loop at the bow, and then back to a fitting on the other side of the cockpit. Pass the line through this last fitting and make it fast upon itself with a stopper knot.

This rig will give you two working lengths. If you only let go of the line, it will be one-third its

length. If you let go of the line and then pull it back through the bow loop and the first fitting by the cockpit, you have use of the full length.

Paddle Float

One hundred and fifty years ago it was recorded that the Aleutian kayakers did not know of, or use, what we now call an Eskimo roll to right a capsized kayak. Instead they would employ the inflated stomach of a sea lion to help them right and reenter their boat. Thankfully you will no longer need to find a suitable animal bladder to do this. Paddle floats in lovely manmade materials are now available.

When modern sea kayakers try to reenter their capsized boats they can inflate a bag-like device, slip it over a paddle blade, and then either jam the other blade under lines that have been specially rigged behind the cockpit or hold it in place. Set up like this the float and paddle act like an outrigger, greatly enhancing the kayak's stability. It is then easier for you to climb up and back into the kayak. Once you're in the boat and it is bailed out, the float can be removed by letting out the air.

Paddle floats are made by a few different companies but all work on the same principle. There are homemade versions using collapsible plastic jugs, which are complicated and probably not worth the risk for the few dollars saved. One alternative is a closed-cell block. This does not need inflating and can be used as a practice aid for braces and rolling.

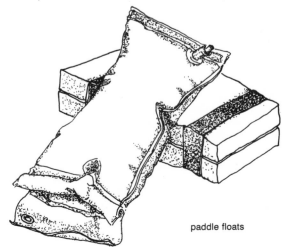

paddle floats

Flotation

The primary idea behind every boat, even a kayak, is to float you, and whatever you put in it. If your kayak (which is probably made of a nonbuoyant material) somehow becomes filled with water (which weighs 64 pounds per cubic foot) it will either sink or flounder hopelessly out of balance, a situation which must be prevented at all costs.

The solution is to exclude water from every unused space. The only place open to water should be where you sit, and even this must be kept to a minimum. Our goal is to stay afloat while in the kayak, even when it is completely flooded. We also want to remain on an even keel and keep the cockpit coaming high enough to prevent more water from coming in. This will require approximately 70 pounds of positive flotation evenly distributed fore and aft.

The most common method of doing this in sea kayaks is by using watertight bulkheads. These may come as standard equipment or as an option and are installed fore and aft of the cockpit. They are made either of fiberglass or foam panels, and are glassed in place or held in with caulking. Almost all caulked bulkheads eventually leak. Check yours at the start of each season and reseal with a polyurethane sealant, if necessary.

Bulkheads create convenient stowage compartments accessible through a variety of hatches. Like bulkheads, hatches also eventually leak. Sometimes simply cleaning the seal, or adding neoprene gaskets will help; sometimes there is just nothing you can do. Luckily the amount they leak is usually very little, but as a backup you might want to keep your gear in watertight bags which in themselves act as reserve buoyancy.

Many boats have no bulkheads or other form of built-in flotation, and will therefore require inflatable flotation bags. These come in a variety of materials, sizes, and shapes, some being able to double as gear stowage bags. Whatever type you use, make sure that they fill up as much space as possible both fore and aft of the cockpit. To do this it will be easier if they are shaped to fit and have extra-long inflating tubes so that they can be inflated in place. Before installing bags check that the inside

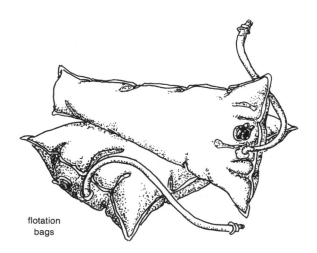

flotation
bags

skin of the kayak has no rough spots and that the bags can be held in place. Inflatable bags belong with collapsible kayaks, too. Even though these boats may have air chambers, they may not have enough buoyancy to float themselves with you in them.

An interesting backup to bulkheads and inflatable bags is the Sea Sock. These are large bags that enclose the lower body and are sealed around the coaming. They tend to feel warm, slippery, and clinging, and take some getting used to. Although they do substantially limit the amount of water that can enter the kayak, they should not be thought of as a primary line of defense.

Eyeglass Strap

Kayakers spend most of their time right-side up, but there will be instances when practicing or by accident you will find yourself in the water. If this happens, make sure you come back up with your glasses on by using one of the many popular straps.

Nose Clips

While practicing, you'll be spending some time underwater, often at unusual angles. Plain, old-fashioned nose clips from a sporting goods or drug store are just the thing to keep your head clear and sinuses free of seaweed.

WHAT YOU WILL NEED

A Place to Learn

Where you learn has a lot of impact on your early success and future abilities. The place you choose should be a sanctuary: a place that you can conveniently return to again and again for practice and working things out. It's your home base. Get your maneuvers right there and you'll be able to take them with you wherever you go.

It is best to learn in an environment similar to that in which you will be doing most of your paddling. Quiet, easily accessible beaches are ideal. Make sure that hard, sharp objects are scarce and that the water is clean, warm (over 65°F), and deepens gradually. Shallow areas (less than 2 feet deep) give a feeling of security when first starting out and are good for experiments in leaning and bracing. A little farther out (at least 4 feet deep) will be perfect for practicing rolling, paddling, and anything else. Try to find a beach protected from the prevailing winds, which bring waves and chills. It's nice to have your car parked nearby as a place to relax, think, and warm up.

Docks, too, are handy for learning. Find one that is low in the water, preferably a floating dock with rubrails around it. A dock in a swimming area or marina could be yours after hours, but be mindful of boat traffic and its resulting wakes.

If you have access to one, a swimming pool can also be a good place to learn. But consider a few things before jumping in. For one, kayaks need to be cleaned before being used in a pool. The little bits of sand, muck, and other debris from the outside world must be removed to preserve the pool's plumbing and health rating. Kayaks and paddles can scratch or otherwise mar the pool and themselves. To prevent this you can use a polyethylene plastic boat, which is less apt to damage itself and its surroundings. As an extra precaution, bumpers, in the form of foam padding, can be duct-taped to bow and stern. You probably won't be able to practice in your own boat because sea kayaks are usually too long and hard to turn in a pool. So you'll more than likely need to find a smaller white water slalom boat.

There's another factor to consider. Emerging from the cloistered haven of a pool to the real world requires a certain amount of relearning, or at least adapting to a new environment. Tides, currents, winds, and weather must all be considered in sea kayaking. If they are present from the beginning, though not so much as to be overwhelming, you'll develop a better sense of what sea kayaking is all about.

This is not to condemn pool sessions. They have a definite place for those whose weather is not always hospitable. In the winter they are godsends for keeping the rust off your hard-won skills. But as soon as the weather breaks it is probably best to go elsewhere. Work done in a pool must supplement, not replace, practice under natural conditions.

Your practice time for specific maneuvers will vary. If you encounter difficulty with what you are doing, stop and return to something familiar. But once comfortable with a maneuver, leave the safety of your practice sanctuary and set out onto open waters to experience what you have learned. If it doesn't feel right, don't push yourself and don't worry, you always have a place to come back to.

MEET YOUR KAYAK

Lifting

Considering how graceful sea kayaks are on the water, it is often surprising how clumsy they can be on land. But, as with almost everything related to this sport, lifting and carrying is more a matter of technique than strength and, once learned, should present no problems.

The easiest method of carrying involves two people, one at each end, using the grab loops, toggles, or ends of the boat. Make sure that all heavy gear has been removed from the boat, especially from the center section.

Carrying a kayak on your own is more difficult, and may even seem hopeless if the boat is heavy. But after a few tries you'll find it can be easily done.

With the boat empty, find the balance point along its length. It should be just a little forward of the seat. Mark this spot on both sides of the cockpit coaming.

To lift, squat down, keeping your feet shoulder-width apart and pointing slightly outward. Make sure your back stays straight. Grab the coaming closest to you with each hand equidistant from the balance point. Pull the boat up against your shins so its side is on the ground. From this position straighten up in one smooth motion. Use your legs to lift, letting the momentum bring your back to the vertical while pulling up slightly with your arms. This will hoist the kayak to waist height, where it can be carried for short distances.

To raise the boat from here onto your shoulder, get an underhand grip on the lower coaming with one hand. Using the hand on the upper coaming as a pivot point, bring the lower hand toward you and upward while simultaneously lifting the boat with the knee and thigh of one leg. If this is done in a rapid and forceful manner you should be able to fling the boat high enough to slip your shoulder under the coaming.

To stabilize the boat while carrying, slide your shoulder slightly behind the balance point. Then bring the hand from your carrying side to the coaming, or somewhere inside the boat, to a position just ahead of the balance point. Use your other hand to guide the boat and keep it from being blown about. Lower the kayak by reversing the procedure, using your raised thigh to help ease it toward the ground.

1

2

3

4

Making It Fit

Manufacturers build their kayaks to accommodate as wide a variety of body types as possible. So it is the rare new boat that provides a perfect fit. As with suits, it is easier to reduce something that is too large than to increase the size of something that's too small. If you have to jam your hips into the seat, or twist your feet and knees outward at excruciatingly oblique angles, get a boat with more room. Conversely, if you feel like a bug in a tub, look for a more compact boat. The initial fit should be at least reasonably close.

Don't be afraid of making adjustments and changes to your boat. If you are careful, you will not irrevocably damage or ruin it. All you'll need is some closed-cell foam (such as Ethafoam, which is used to pack electronics—or Ensulite, sometimes known as EVA, which is used for campers' sleeping pads), a knife, hacksaw, sandpaper, and adhesive. For fiberglass boats, plain contact cement is fine. Polyethylene plastic boats may need special adhesives, so ask the dealer or builder first.

The purpose of a good fit is to provide comfort, give control, and improve efficiency by transmitting the forces generated by the body/paddle combination directly to the boat. You want to be able to make solid contact with your feet, knees, hips, rear, and back. The fit should be loose enough for comfort, yet close enough so that by flexing your feet and thighs you become one with the kayak.

The balls of your feet are the direct transmitters of forward forces from the body/paddle to the kayak. Adjust the foot pedals or bar so that your knees are touching the underside of the deck and your lower back, from the waist down, is gently pressed into the back of the seat. Heels should be close together, toes turned outward, and feet at not quite 90 degrees to your ankles. Sit this way for fifteen minutes. If your feet or legs go to sleep, readjust to give yourself more room.

Balancing and leaning forces are directed through the knees. The farther apart you can place your knees, without being uncomfortable, the better your side-to-side balancing will be. They should just touch the deck near the sides of the boat. If their angle feels comfortable, and not cramped or awkward, place some thin pad-

ding on the underside of the deck as a cushion. If they do not make contact with the deck, add thick pieces of foam as spacers. Tape the foam into place first and paddle that way for a while before gluing. In addition to your knees, some boats let you brace the upper part of your thighs against the coaming. These may also need some padding.

Your hips help you control and balance the boat, functions they can best fulfill if you are not sliding around on the seat. To keep yourself in place, put foam blocks between your hips and the side of the boat. Do not pack yourself in so tightly that you have trouble getting in or out of the boat, or that an extra layer of clothing will affect the fit. Leave an extra 1/2 to 3/4 inch on either side.

Pressing your feet and legs forward will be for naught if there is nothing to stop you from sliding backward. Both the seat and the back support help you lock yourself in and transmit the body/paddle forces that stop, slow, or reverse the boat. Back supports usually take the form of a seatback or cushioned strap. It should be no higher than necessary and is not to be thought of as a backrest on which to relax. If your boat's seatback extends too far above your lower back, it will restrict upper body motion and should be changed.

Finally we come to the seat, which hopefully is giving cushioned support to your body. A seat should be as low as possible to gain overall stability, but not so low as to be detrimental to your paddling. It should provide friction to keep you from sliding around and should be sloped at the same angle as your thighs to give them support. It would be nice if it were soft, too.

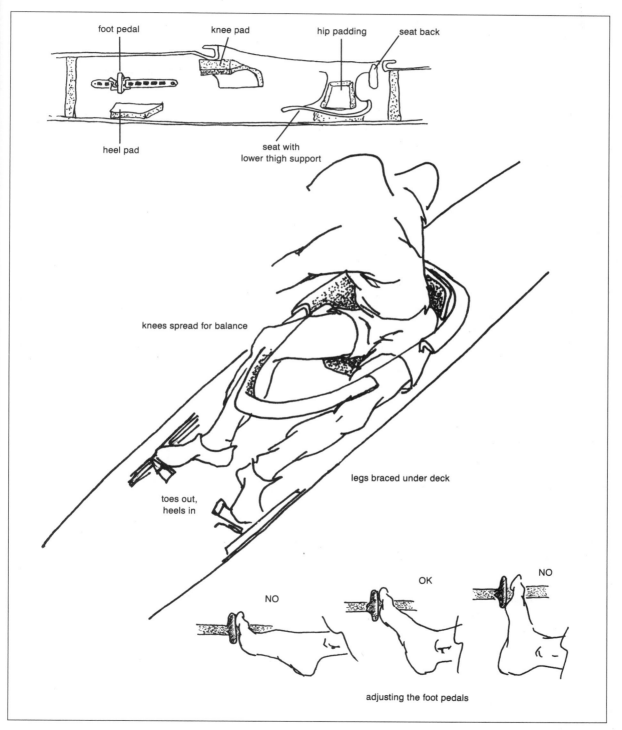

foot pedal

knee pad

hip padding

seat back

heel pad

seat with
lower thigh support

knees spread for balance

legs braced under deck

toes out,
heels in

NO

OK

NO

adjusting the foot pedals

MEET YOUR KAYAK

Transporting

Hoisting a 60-pound kayak onto your cartop need not be a snatch-and-lift motion. Instead of lifting it all at once, do it in stages, starting from the ground or a shoulder carry.

Depending on your car's shape, you can put the kayak on from behind or from the side. When coming from the rear, place the kayak on the ground so that four feet of its bow is off to one side and the stern is directly behind the car. Put a towel or blanket under the stern if you want to prevent scratches. Lift the bow and place it on the rear rack. Walk to the stern to lift and push the boat into place. If the boat does not slide easily, you will have to advance it by lifting and moving in short stages. Be patient and you'll do it.

For the side lift, place the boat about four feet from the car so that the bow extends beyond the front rack by approximately six feet. Lift the bow onto the front rack. If only a short length makes it on, lift the kayak by its middle section to get it farther forward. When set, lift the stern into place. Once your kayak is up you have to keep it there. To do this the boat has to be supported from underneath and secured in place at its middle and ends.

Ideally, support should come from a rack with either horizontal cradles which distribute the weight and are low enough to make loading easy; or vertical "J" cradles or stacker bars that require you to lift the boat higher but let it rest on its side, its strongest point. An alternative for short trips is thick, resilient padding over a cross bar. Regardless of the type, racks should be as close to five feet apart as possible. This spreads support and keeps the widest section of the kayak between the tie-down points to prevent slipping.

Tie downs that cross over the boat are best if they are straps. These minimize chafe and distribute their hold over a wider area than rope. When used with self-locking, cam-type buckles an amazingly tight and tenacious grip can be achieved. But don't overdo it. You could crack a fiberglass boat, deform a polyethylene plastic one, or make a mess out of coamings and hatches by overtightening.

Nylon or Dacron rope, not bungie cords (too stretchy) or polypropylene rope (too slippery), should be used for tying the ends of the kayak to prevent lifting and lateral movement. Lines should form an inverted "V" from the kayak's ends to each side of the front and back of the car. The best knots for this job are the bowline, which makes a fixed loop that will not jam, and a stopper knot, which makes an adjustable loop to provide tension. Lines should be attached to the kayak and then to any point on the car that will not chafe through the rope. Cars without bumpers can often close straps under their hoods or trunk lids leaving enough sticking out that loops tied in them give something to fasten ropes to.

Keep cartopped kayaks empty of heavy equipment, facing forward, and closed to the elements. Gear can fly out at high speeds, or its weight, as well as the weight of collected rain, can strain the boat as it bounces down the road. Even cockpit covers can blow off and should be secured with a safety line just in case.

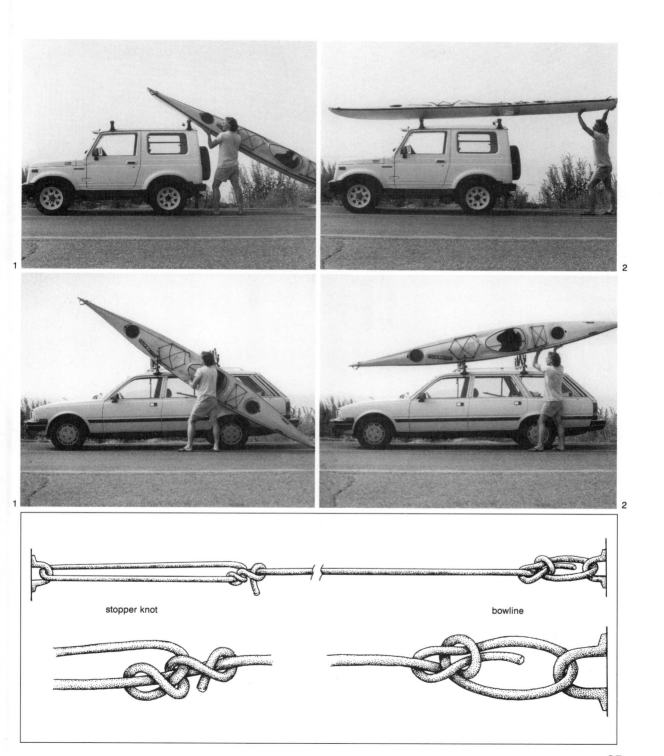

stopper knot

bowline

GETTING IN AND OUT (DRY)

Beach: Kayak in Water

Your center of gravity is at its highest in relation to the kayak when getting in or out. So there's no wonder that the kayak, and you, are most unstable during these procedures. This is where most beginners take their first dunking.

To avoid this, use the paddle as a stabilizing bar, sort of like an eight-foot-long kickstand. It's easy to do, but if you are feeling a little anxious or clumsy, you might first try the procedure on a grassy lawn to prove to yourself that it really works.

This type of entry and exit requires the kayak to be close-in and parallel to shore. If the wind is blowing onto the beach with any strength, or if there is excessive wave action, you will have to forgo this procedure and use the kayak-on-land technique.

Before starting put on all your protective clothing, then the spray skirt if you're using one, and finally your PFD. Roll up the back hem of the skirt so you won't sit on it. With the kayak afloat in six inches of calm water to minimize damage to its bottom, bring it alongside the beach. Stand in the water between the boat and the shore facing the bow. Place your paddle behind your back and lay its shaft across the boat's aft deck, just behind the coaming and perpendicular to the boat's centerline. The boatside blade should be just past the side of the kayak, the shoreside blade resting flat on the beach. To prevent damage, the power face of curved blades resting on the shore should face upward.

Using the hand closest to the boat, hold the paddle shaft against the aft coaming with your fingers inside the coaming and your thumb around the shaft. Place the hand closest to the shore on the shaft just outboard of the boat's side, using the same sort of backhanded grip. As much as possible avoid placing too much strain on the paddle. It should only have to take the minimum amount of weight necessary for you to keep your balance.

With the paddle in position, sit down on the aft deck. Bring one leg in at a time while leaning toward shore to prevent tipping. Depending on the size of your cockpit, you now either: lower your rear down to the seat with your knees bent; or work your legs under the deck until they are far enough in so you can lower your rear onto the seat.

Once in, bring the paddle around front, secure it so it won't float off, and then snap on your spray skirt. To exit the kayak, repeat the procedure in reverse.

Beach: Kayak on Land

There will be times when the water is too rough or the bottom drops away too abruptly for you to be able to get into the boat while it is in the water. When this happens you will have to get in on land and "walk" the kayak, with you in it, to the water.

Since you'll want to keep your walk as short as possible, it is best to put the boat down as close to the waterline as possible. This might be an area in the surf's wash or a spot where the bow is at least in the water. Naturally you'll be facing bow out, perpendicular to the beach; and naturally you'll pick as soft a spot as possible for the sake of your boat's bottom.

If you're still feeling wary about your kayak, or have a boat that is tippy even on land, and some V-bottomed boats are, you can steady the boat by using your paddle as a brace. If this is not necessary, you can either: step right in and sit down; support your weight with your hands on the aft coaming and bring your legs in one at a time; or sit on the aft deck and do the same thing. Be careful with this last method as some polyethylene plastic boats may be dented (but should pop right back) if too much weight is put on the deck. Whichever way you use to get in, you might want to knock off as much sand or mud as possible before bringing your feet into the boat. It's always better not to be sitting in grit.

Once in, with the spray skirt in place, you can begin your march to the sea. But before doing anything make sure that you secure your paddle. Then, using your fists, reach down with both hands and push. At the same time try to bring your knees up and swing yourself forward. In this turtle-like fashion you will eventually reach the water with a minimum amount of scarring to your boat.

Some find using their fists uncomfortable. If that's the case, you can curl your knuckles in like an orangutan and walk on them. Try to avoid the more human-like way of using your outspread hands to do the pushing. Although it seems the more logical approach, it may actually be putting an unnecessary strain on your wrists.

If your arms are not long enough for this sort of travel, you can use your fist, or knuckles, on one side and the paddle on the other. Your fist will take most of the weight while the paddle acts like a cane for the opposite side.

You'll want to get yourself afloat as fast and completely as possible. If you don't, there is a chance of being hung up with your bow in the water and stern on land, which is a very unstable position. If caught like this, push or paddle your way into deeper water, and be ready to brace with your paddle.

GETTING IN AND OUT (DRY)

Low Dock

As populations grow and beach access decreases, more of us will be doing our kayaking from public launching ramps. If your ramp area isn't crowded or its surface too rough, you could get in and out of the boat as if from a beach. But if the place is popular, or you don't want to grind your paddle blade to splinters on the concrete, you'll need to know how to use a dock. Since launching ramps are meant for smaller boats, docks there are usually low to the water.

To a kayak, a low dock is anything that is close to, or below, coaming level. With a dock, or anything else, of this height you can use the paddle as a supporting brace.

Start by sitting as close to the edge of the dock as possible facing the bow of the boat. Put the paddle behind you, laying the shaft across the boat's aft deck just to the rear of the coaming. The outboard blade should be just past the side of the boat and the other blade resting flat on the dock, with the power face up for curved blades. Hold the paddle shaft against the coaming and place your other hand on the dock. Try to put as little weight on the shaft as possible. With most of your weight supported by your legs and the hand on the dock, bring one leg in at a time, and then lower yourself onto the seat.

There are also techniques that do not use a paddle for support. One starts in the seated position as above. Keep the paddle nearby so it can be reached once you're in. Put both feet on the centerline. Use your arms to lift you off the dock, swing your rear over the boat, and lower yourself onto the seat. Your upper body weight must be kept over the dock and supported by your arms during the procedure.

Another way is to squat down near the edge of the dock facing the bow of the boat. While supporting yourself with your legs and the hand on the dock, take hold of the front coaming. Keeping your weight over the dock, swing the leg closest to the boat into the cockpit, putting your foot just to the far side of the centerline. Now, with most of your weight over the hand on the dock, swing the other leg into the boat and settle down onto the seat.

All three procedures are equally valid. It's your choice. The size or shape of some cockpits may make it impossible to lower yourself directly onto the seat. When this occurs, place your feet in the cockpit as before, but this time lower your rear to the aft deck. Once seated there, lift up a little, straighten your legs, and wriggle down onto the seat.

No matter how you get in, remember to roll up the back of your spray skirt before entering the boat. Trying to reach behind to get it out from under you could result in a dunking. Do this slowly and carefully.

Exiting the kayak is simply a matter of reversing these procedures. But you might find that the technique that worked best to get you into the boat may not necessarily be the one you'll use to get out. Experiment.

paddle as brace

from seated position

from squatting position

High Dock

To a kayak, a high dock is anything above coaming level. This means that it is too far above the boat for you to either lean over and steady it or to use your paddle as a supporting brace. Anything over three to four feet from the water is too high. The determining factor is how far up you can comfortably reach while seated in the boat.

To gauge the probability for success of an entry from a high dock, sit on the very edge and hang your legs over the side. If you have to stretch to make your toes reach the cockpit floor, you're flirting with trouble and should try to find some place lower. For a dock that is within your range though, getting in and out may take a little effort but should not be all that difficult.

First, put your paddle down so you can reach it when in the boat. Then sit on the edge of the dock with your feet holding the kayak in place. Twist your body so you are facing the bow, place both hands on the dock ahead and slightly to one side, push up so as to lift your rear, and then roll over on your front. Now, with your body leaning over the dock, rear suspended over the boat, and feet on the centerline of the cockpit, slowly lower yourself onto the seat bending your knees as you descend.

During this procedure keep as much weight on your hands as possible. Trying to support too much weight with your feet will cause the boat to move, leaving you hanging in space.

The cockpits of some boats may make it impossible to lower yourself directly onto the seat. When this occurs, place your feet in the cockpit as before, but lower your rear to the aft deck. Once seated there, lift up a little, straighten your legs, and wriggle down onto the seat.

To get out of the boat you use the same procedure in reverse. The only problem you might encounter is that your arms may not be strong enough to pull yourself up. If this is the case, bring your knees up so your feet are near your rear end or get up on to the aft deck with your feet in the cockpit. From this position your legs can help a little. But don't try to stand. This will cause the boat to go one way and you another. Let your arms do most of the work. If you can manage to get your upper torso over the edge of the dock it will be possible to drag the rest of you behind it. Not very elegant, but it works.

The higher the dock, the more you will have to rely on your sense of balance and the strength of your arms. Consider wind and waves, too. It might be worth going a little out of your way to find a slightly lower dock.

1

2

GETTING OUT AND IN (WET)

Wet Exit

To those who have never experienced it, the prospect of a capsize may conjure fears of being trapped upside down underwater. But once it happens the reality is almost a let-down. There's nothing to it.

The fact is that in a properly-fitted kayak you are held in by the pressure of your feet, thighs, and hips against the boat. Relax this pressure and, in most boats, when you're upside down you'll almost fall out. The worst that can happen is that you'll get water up your nose, which can easily be prevented with a pair of nose clips.

Practice wet exits in water that is at least four feet deep, wearing your PFD, and with a friend standing nearby, if only for moral support. For these first attempts do not bother with a spray skirt or your paddle.

Once upside down try to relax, using pressure from your legs to hold you in. Force yourself to bang on the bottom of the boat three times or do anything else that will postpone a hasty escape. The complete exit takes only two seconds, while the average person can hold his breath for thirty. So time is on your side.

To exit place both hands on the kayak next to your hips, ease the grip of your legs and straighten them to help you slip out, use your arms to push, and curl forward as in a somersault. Once up, immediately grab the kayak. Never let yourself get separated from it.

Now try the same thing with a spray skirt in place. When putting it on make sure that the release strap is readily accessible. Practice releasing the skirt while upright. Then go out and capsize, hang there to collect your thoughts, pull and lift the release strap, check the skirt to see that it has released, then roll out as before. There may come a time when the release strap is missing or mistakenly tucked under. To get free, lean to one side, grab the bunched up material on that side, and lift it away from the coaming.

Next try an exit with your paddle. Capsize while holding it in both hands. Once upside down hold on with one hand, using the other to deal with the skirt and pushing out from the boat. Come to the surface with the paddle and grab the kayak. Never let either go adrift.

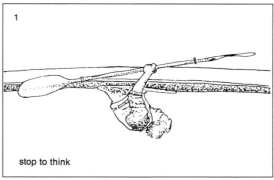

1

stop to think

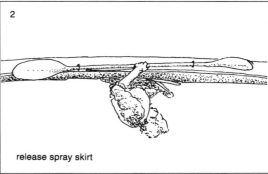

2

release spray skirt

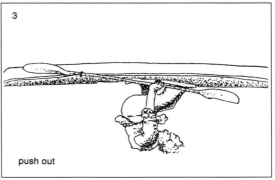

3

push out

4

hold on to paddle and kayak

GETTING OUT AND IN (WET)

Swimming

While swimming with the kayak is not a common activity, it is something that must be learned. If for some reason you find yourself out of the boat, the most desirable option is usually to get back in. But sometimes this is not possible or, if you are very close to shore, even desirable.

Before learning to swim with a kayak there are some basic rules of safety to keep in mind.

First, and most important, is that you should be able to swim at least 200 feet on your own. Every paddler must be a reasonably good swimmer. You need not have great style or be able to swim long distances, just be good enough to feel confident in and under the water. No matter how accomplished a swimmer you might be, it is almost always safest to stick with the boat in case of an emergency. A kayak, even partially swamped, will provide extra flotation and be easier to spot than a lone swimmer.

There is also the nature of kayaks to consider. Partially-flooded kayaks can often drift much faster than you would expect and a gentle breeze can push an empty one well ahead of even the best swimmer. So always keep hold of your boat and, when you must let go, stay on its downwind side. There is an exception to this rule and that is when in surf or breaking seas. During these times try to maintain your hold while staying up wind or wave of the boat so it won't hit you. No matter what the sea's condition, you'll be best off if you keep a capsized kayak inverted until you are ready to bail it out or get back in. A swamped kayak that is right side up is inherently unstable and susceptible to taking on more water. By keeping it upside down you will minimize the amount of water that can be collected in the boat while maintaining an air pocket that improves buoyancy.

With these points in mind, try some swimming. Always wear a PFD and make sure that your boat is suitably equipped with flotation. Paddle out to deep water, capsize, wet exit, and surface, holding the boat by the coaming and keeping a grip on the paddle. Now swim to the bow of the inverted kayak and get hold of some solid fitting. Lifting toggles are ideal for this, but be careful of large grab loops. In rough water a swamped kayak can spin around its long axis. If your hands or fingers are in a loop when this happens, they might become trapped.

Transfer the paddle to the same hand that is holding the boat and strike out for shore using a back or side stroke. If in the process you have lost hold of the paddle, stay with the kayak and swim it and yourself to the paddle. Paddles drift very slowly, kayaks very swiftly. Also make sure when practicing, and in all future outings, that your equipment is securely stowed.

There are some paddlers who like to tie a line between the paddle and the boat or themselves. This paddle leash is intended to keep the paddle from drifting off, and leaves hands free to work on other tasks. The idea is sound, but there is a danger that the leash can get tangled around you or the boat. So, for the sake of safety, make sure that the leash can be easily released from the paddle and that you disconnect it when in turbulent water that might capsize or spin the kayak.

Emptying

A kayak with water in it is more than a damp annoyance. It's unsafe. With sea water weighing 64 pounds per cubic foot, and fresh water at 62, it doesn't take much of it to drastically reduce a kayak's ability to float. That same water, given free access to slosh around, can make a boat very unstable. It becomes obvious then that you'll want to empty a swamped kayak as soon as you can.

To make life safer, and put the odds in your favor, you must be sure that your boat is fitted with adequate flotation in both ends. Secured air bags are good, bulkheads and waterproof hatches even better. Most single kayaks fitted with bulkheads take on and retain a surprisingly small amount of water in their cockpits. Kayaks with no flotation can take on surprisingly great amounts of water and are not averse to sinking. Always take along something to bail with: a sponge, pump, or scoop.

If you are very close to shore, it may be a wise option to wait and empty the boat there. This is especially true if the water is very cold. Emptying a boat in deep water can take quite a bit of time, and if it's cold, you'll want to avoid hypothermia by spending as little time as possible in that water.

If the shoreline is attainable, not too rocky or rough, put the stern of the inverted kayak on land and lift the bow. If the shoreline is inhospitable, stand in the shallows with the stern in deep water and lift the bow clear. In a bulkheaded boat most of the water will collect in the forward end of the cockpit. Empty this first. Once most of the water has drained, turn the boat over and sponge or pump out the rest.

Initially you may experience some difficulty in getting the boat free from the water because of suction around the cockpit opening. To relieve this, tilt the boat on its side until the cockpit rim clears the surface, breaking the seal. While still in this position, lift slowly and carefully to let as much water drain from the cockpit as possible before bringing the kayak to land. Putting the weight of a fully waterlogged boat on land can break both its back and yours.

For some boats you will have to lift and drain one end and then the other. This may have to be repeated a number of times. In all of the above situations you may need to support one side of the boat to keep the boat fully inverted while draining. Lift with your legs not your back.

When you have to empty a boat in deep water there are a number of ways to go about it, though one seems to be more effective and reliable than the others. With the kayak inverted, swim up next to the cockpit. While holding onto your paddle with one hand, reach under the boat with the other and grab the cockpit coaming on the opposite side. With a quick motion pull this hand toward you while pushing up on the near side with the hand holding the paddle. This will smartly flip the boat upright and, if done fast enough, bring very little water aboard. Reenter the boat using a paddle float or the help of a companion. Bail out the remaining water and get underway.

Paddle Float Reentry

Your first attempts to get back into the kayak after a capsize might result in a startling realization. The boat, which was a little wobbly while you were in it, has now become an unpredictable demon.

There are sea kayaks stable enough to climb back into without outside help. To see if yours is one of these, try this experiment: With the boat upright and you in the water, slide up onto the aft deck facing the bow. Stay on your stomach while pulling yourself forward. When over the cockpit sit up with both legs in the water and spread out for stability. Lower your rear onto the seat and then bring your legs in. If that doesn't work, try sliding up from the middle of the boat onto the rear deck face down, inserting both legs into the cockpit, twisting around, and then lowering yourself onto the seat. Ten to one says you won't make it.

Even if you do, don't feel too sure of yourself. What might work in calm water when you're feeling fit, may not do the job when it's blowing and you are tired, maybe even a little frightened.

For the lone paddler attempting an unassisted rescue, using a paddle float is the most reliable reentry method. This system puts a float on one end of the paddle while the other end is held to the boat creating a stability-enhancing outrigger. For those who can climb aboard in calm water, the float system is a good back-up. For those whose boats are tippy, the paddle float may be your only hope of getting back into the kayak. Mind you, the paddle float is not a panacea or the ultimate rescue procedure; but it has been proven to have a high success rate in a wide variety of situations. The one place it is guaranteed to fail, and should never be attempted, is inside the surfline. Never attempt any reentry rescue here; instead, swim or drift to shore where you can contemplate your next move in safety.

The paddle float reentry requires preparation in order to be effective. First, the boat should be prepared with special rigging, then you have to be prepared with practice.

To rig your kayak it will have to have a relatively flat area just behind the cockpit and a series of strong bungie cords or taut straps over this area. The objective is to firmly hold the paddle perpendicular to the boat. Another part of the rigging is a place to stow the float. When considering a location make sure that after a capsize the float will be easy to get at and not be separated from you. Most paddlers stow their floats on the aft deck under bungie cords. When doing so, tie a short line from the float to the kayak to prevent accidental loss. If your float is the inflatable kind, you might want to consider keeping it partially filled so you will only have to top it off once in the water.

When practicing remember that in a real situation you will probably be doing this because all else has failed or no outside help is available. So rehearse the procedures often and in varying conditions. Develop a set routine

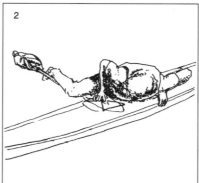

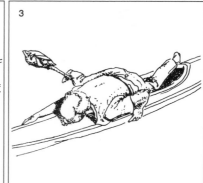

that you can follow by numbers. Remember: Practice prevents panic. Here's how it goes.

- After capsizing, right the boat. Try to keep as much water out as you can, but do not bail it out at this time. Your first goal is to get out of the water.

- Move to the downwind side of the boat and put the paddle float on one of the blades. If you are using a foam block, just slip it in place. If you are using an inflatable float, put it on the blade first, then inflate it.

- Place the other blade under the retaining rigging on the rear deck.

- Staying forward of the paddle shaft, hoist yourself onto the aft deck with one leg resting on the paddle for support. Stay face down, keep low to the boat, do not get up on hands or elbows, and keep most of your weight on the boat, favoring the float side. Although your PFD may seem a hindrance during these contortions, do not give in to the temptation to remove it.

- Place the nearest leg into the cockpit. Maintain the face down position, keep your weight leaning toward the float. Now put the second leg in.

- Keeping your weight toward the float, rotate to face upward and slide forward onto the seat.

- Leaning towards the float, bail out as much water as you can, put your spray skirt in place, and, if need be, pump out the rest.

- Take your paddle out of the rigging and remove the float. This can be precarious. Go slowly, cautiously, and wait for a lull in the wind or waves.

There may be times when you find yourself in a boat that is not rigged for a paddle float re-entry. This does not mean that you can't use the system, only that it will be more difficult. The following procedure requires more dexterity and strength, while providing less control and stability.

After swimming to the downwind side of the upright boat, slip the float over one of the paddle's blades, inflate it if necessary, and locate yourself aft of the cockpit. Hold the paddle shaft against the rear of the coaming with the hand closest to the cockpit. While holding the paddle in position, climb aboard the aft deck with one leg on the paddle shaft. Hoist yourself further up onto the boat while keeping your weight toward the float side. Swing your body around and bring one leg into the cockpit and then the other. As before, rotate to a face up position, slide onto the seat, and secure the boat.

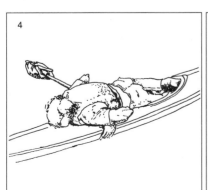

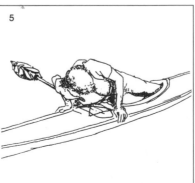

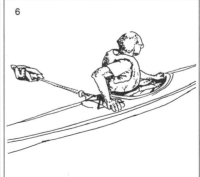

EXPLORING YOUR LIMITS

Stability

A sailboat gets stability from ballast deep *below* the waterline, giving it a low center of gravity. As the boat heels, the ballast provides a constant righting force to keep from capsizing.

A kayak is just the opposite. Its center of gravity is relatively high, being a substantial distance *above* the waterline. Since this isn't going to help matters much, we have to look elsewhere to get stability. And the best place we'll find it is in the movement of our bodies. This is called dynamic stability, and when you know how to use it, it's better than ballast.

Here's the theory: You and your kayak have a combined center of gravity somewhere near your waistline that is the concentration of forces pushing downward. The forces pushing upward that keep you afloat are concentrated at a spot called the center of buoyancy.

Predictably, these two forces work against each other. But what adds spice to the equation is that while the center of gravity is always located near your belly button, the position of the center of buoyancy changes as the boat tilts, making it infinitely variable.

When the boat is level the center of gravity is directly above the center of buoyancy. In this condition the forces are balanced and you stay upright. If you and the boat lean over, the center of gravity and center of buoyancy will move outwards, but at different rates. As long as the upward force is farther to the side than the downward force, the boat will want to stay upright. Unfortunately you don't have to lean

too far before just the opposite happens, whereupon you invert to a stable position very much like a sailboat's ballasted keel.

Capsizing is almost guaranteed if you try to hold your upper body perpendicular to the boat when it tilts. In this position the center of gravity moves rapidly to the side. To avoid this all you have to do is to hold your upper body perpendicular to the water, not the boat. This keeps your center of gravity in a more stable position closer to the boat's center of buoyancy. As the boat, the upward force, tilts one way, your upper body, the downward force, compensates and tilts the other. That's dynamic stability.

Here's how it's done: The secret is to stay loose and be able to bend sideways just above your hips. By relaxing your stomach muscles you can separate your upper body from the boat, which is being firmly gripped by your lower body. This separation lets the boat do what it wants. It can wiggle, wobble, or flop around. As long as your upper body remains steady and upright, you'll be OK. It happens almost automatically.

Try this to get the feel of it. Hold your paddle horizontally in front of you. Rock the kayak by alternately lifting one knee while pushing down with the opposite buttock. Keep your body vertical. You'll see that it won't take long before you are increasing the angle of the boat far beyond what you thought would be possible. Your only limitation will be how much movement your hips and waist will allow.

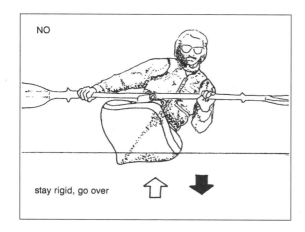

NO

stay rigid, go over

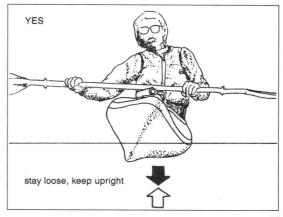

YES

stay loose, keep upright

Balance

While the main objective of this lesson is to explore balance, both the kayak's and yours, there will also be some side benefits. You're likely to find that you instinctively know more about kayaking than you might have thought. Unlike other lessons, this one has no right or wrong way, no musts, shoulds, or have tos. This is about doing, not reading; sensing, not intellectualizing. Educators may call it "Discovery Learning," but it's just fooling around.

To build a foundation of confidence for the techniques that will follow, you will need to develop a feel for the natural balance of you and your boat. To do that you're going to have to get wet, and yes, have fun.

Find a place where the water's warm and protected, put on a nose clip, and make like a polar bear with a beach ball. Be careful though. If you're in a limited area like a pool, watch out for swimmers, other playing paddlers, and the sides of the pool. Be sure to stay in water at least four feet deep so you won't be banging your head on the bottom.

For those who have forgotten what it's like to be playful, here are some ideas on how to explore your boat's balance:

Climb into the boat from the water. First over the rear deck, then from the side. Now try to climb out of the boat. Straddle the cockpit, sit on the rear deck with your feet in the cockpit, stand up, lay down. . .

Try to swamp the boat completely (make sure it has flotation so it won't sink on you). You may be surprised at how little water a boat with bulkheads will take on. Now try to get into the boat from the water, and then from a dock or pool side. Paddle around in it with your hands. Now empty out half of the water and try the same things. Take particular notice of how the amount of water in the boat affects its stability and performance.

Find the point at which the boat capsizes. In the shallows (less than one foot) of a protected beach tilt the boat over towards the shore, supporting yourself with your hand. Lean over a little, then a little more. You'll be surprised how far over you can go. Try it on both sides. The same can be done holding on to the side of a pool or dock.

While in the boat try to bend over and "kiss" the water. See how low you can bend before going over.

Paddle with your hands, paddle with one hand, spin the boat around, go forward, backward, and figure out how to make it go sideways. Sit on the rear deck and paddle. If the cockpit is large enough kneel in it and paddle.

Capsize the boat and swim underwater to bring your head up in the cockpit. Look around and see for yourself how little water collects in

an upside-down kayak.

Invert the boat, crawl over it from one side to the other, and then return underwater.

Have a water fight with another paddler without using paddles. Try to fill the other boat to the point that it becomes unstable.

Become a member of the dry hair club by getting out of a capsizing boat before it goes completely over.

Experiment, make up your own games, and don't be embarrassed. The whole idea of kayaking is to have fun. And if it's any conciliation to your ego, there are very few top paddlers who haven't at one time or another just fooled around with their boats. The more familiar you become with your kayak the easier the whole learning process will be; and the more relaxed you are in your boat and on the water the better your technique will be. So lighten up and explore the balance.

PADDLING

Holding the Paddle

Paddling is fundamental to, and the essence of, sea kayaking. Right from the start you must develop a sense of what a good paddle stroke is and then evolve one that is right for you. Your goal is to find a style that is efficient enough to carry you long distances and comfortable enough to be maintained for hours. To achieve this you will have to make many choices along the way, the first being how you hold your paddle.

Where on the shaft you put your hands is completely up to you. Their position affects, and is responsive to, your stroke. And, since your stroke will vary, so will the position of your hands. For maximum power to accelerate, maneuver, or push into a strong current or headwind, use a wide grip. This is like low gear on a car, giving a slower but more powerful stroke. If you bring your hands closer together you get a higher gearing, with more blade motion for less arm movement. This is used to sustain a cruising speed or for fast traveling in calm conditions.

To effectively shift gears you have to know the range of hand grips. You can determine the outer limits of your grip by holding the paddle over your head, making a right angle with your elbows so your forearms are vertical and upper arms horizontal. This is the position for maximum low gear. Mark the shaft with tape just outside your small fingers, making sure that the marks are equal distances from the center. To find the limit for high gear bring the shaft up to your shoulders with your upper arms against your sides. Mark the shaft near your thumbs.

Your effective grip range is between the marks. For now, pick any spot within this range that feels comfortable.

How the paddle is gripped will be determined by which hand you choose to be your control hand. With feathered paddles the control hand holds the shaft to allow wrist and forearm motion to produce the proper blade-to-water angle for each stroke. This hand is fixed to the shaft and never changes its grip. The other hand keeps a loose hold on the shaft, allowing it to rotate freely. Either hand can be used for control. With non-feathered paddles both hands simultaneously perform the control function.

The control hand holds the shaft so the top of the nearest blade lines up with the top row of your knuckles. Maintain that grasp so you'll always know the angle of the blade in relation to your hand. Blade angle in relation to the water is changed by moving your wrists or forearms, not by loosening your grip and turning the shaft. Once you lose your grip you lose your orientation to the blade, making the blade's angle a constant guessing game.

Don't keep a death grip on the shaft, there's no need for it, and it will only bring discomfort. Hold the shaft in the curve of your fingers, with most of the gripping done by the thumb and forefinger. Keep a light and responsive hold. It may seem too delicate, but your fist will automatically tighten up when needed, so don't worry. A relaxed natural grip gives you a longer stroke and reduces lateral wrist movements that can stress tendons.

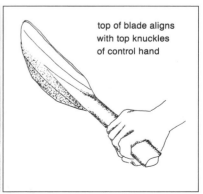

top of blade aligns with top knuckles of control hand

Basic Stroke: Non-Feathered

A non-feathered paddle has its blades set parallel to one another and requires a minimum of shaft rotation. A feathered paddle has its blades set from 75 to 90 degrees to one another and requires shaft rotation for each blade to meet the water at the desired angle. The choice between the two is subjective. The success you have with one over the other has more to do with what your body is comfortable with and using proper technique than anything else.

Find out which you feel most at ease with. To do this use a take-apart paddle that lets you switch from non-feathered, to either right- or left-hand controlled feathered. For this lesson set the blades for non-feathered.

All paddling is a complex cycle of separate components that build upon each other. Within each stroke there is a pushing and pulling of opposing arms, wrist motion, and twisting of the body. Start with the basic pulling motion of the arms.

You may want to take your inaugural strokes on land, or in hip-deep water to add a touch of authenticity and resistance as you pull on the blade. When you're ready to try it in a boat, head for an open stretch of protected water, not a pool. You'll need a lot of room to paddle so you can have time to make mistakes, correct them, and get a feel for what you are doing.

When in the boat wedge your knees against the deck, and put light pressure on the foot braces to hold your lower back snugly against its support. Don't slouch, keep your head up and eyes on the horizon. Hold the shaft away from you at chest height, arms slightly bent, with elbows pointing out and down.

You can start off on either side, but for the sake of demonstrating, begin on the right. Extend your right arm so it is straight; keep your left hand held close-in, up around your shoulder. Place the blade gently in the water making a clean entry with no splashing. To get a good long stroke you'll want to set the blade in as far forward as possible without having to lean forward. You can extend your reach, and reduce wrist strain, by straightening your last three fingers so the shaft is momentarily being

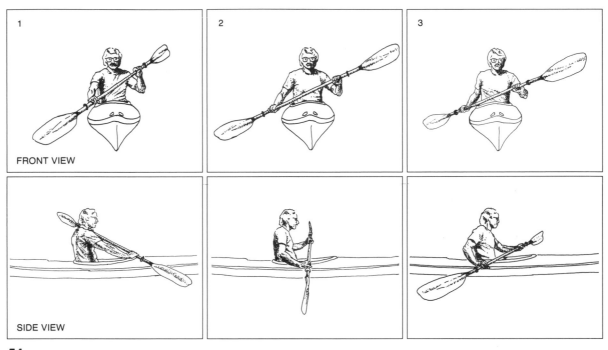

1

2

3

FRONT VIEW

SIDE VIEW

held by the thumb and forefinger. Aim for a spot near your foot and put the blade in close to the boat. Immerse the blade almost to its throat but no deeper, and try to maintain this depth throughout the stroke.

To help you envision the forces involved, think of the blade as being inserted into something solid while you pull yourself, and the kayak you are attached to, toward it. You are not pulling the blade back through the water as it might appear.

Only after the blade is completely immersed can power be applied by your right arm. As it comes back, your left hand simultaneously goes forward as if making a diagonal punch toward the bow, without crossing the centerline of the boat. The palm of the left hand faces forward with fingers relaxed. The shaft angle should be kept comfortably flat. This way the blade in the air is less apt to be caught by the wind, drips will not find their way to you, and the stroke will provide support as well as propulsion. Your left hand will have most of the responsibility for shaft angle. Let it go no higher than eye level.

Throughout the pull be aware of the blade's angle to the water. It should stay close to vertical. If its top tilts toward the bow of the kayak, the blade will want to dig deeper. If its top tilts toward the stern, the blade will want to lift out.

Maximum power should be exerted as your knees are passing the blade. Once your hips are level with the blade the forward thrust of the stroke diminishes. This should coincide with your left hand being at the limit of its forward reach. So ease off on the pull and lift the blade up with a brisk slicing motion. After the blade is out, keep raising your right hand until it assumes a similar position to your left hand at the beginning of the stroke. This directs the left hand blade forward and down toward the water so it is ready to start the stroke on the left side.

Once you've mastered the separate elements, concentrate on having a smooth continuous action. If you think about it too much you'll only get confused. Use your brain each time you put the blade in and take it out. Let your body fill in the rest. Hold down the pace while learning, throwing in an occasional sprint for excitement.

Basic Stroke: Feathered

To the basic arm pull used on a non-feathered paddle, you will now add the wrist motion needed for feathered paddling.

At this point many novices inwardly say, "Why bother with feathering now? I'll just use a non-feathered paddle to learn the basics and make a decision between the two later." You could, but you wouldn't be giving yourself a fair chance. Since you are eventually going to have to choose, don't be tempted to stay with non-feathering because of a preconceived notion that feathered paddling is more complex or difficult. It's not, but you'll have to prove that to yourself. Give it time, and it will soon become obvious which feels more natural. When this happens, make your decision and stick with it. From there on don't vacillate from one to the other. This will only confuse you and delay the ultimate refining of your stroke. When ambivalent, go with feathering first. If you find it's not for you, it will be easier to switch over to non-feathering than the other way around.

Now for another choice. Which will be your controlling hand? The control hand uses wrist and forearm motion to rotate the shaft so that each blade meets the water at the desired angle. Its grip on the shaft remains constant,

the top edge of the nearest blade lining up with the top row of your knuckles. The other hand keeps a loose hold, acting only as a guide.

Curiously, most people, whether left- or right-handed, seem to prefer right-hand control. You'll probably know which is best for you after a few trial strokes. Since you've got a take-apart paddle, experiment. But once again, you'll eventually have to pick a control hand and stick with it.

To start, it will be instructive to see what the control hand really does. Hold the paddle in front of you with your control hand properly positioned and your arms almost straight. When the control-side blade is vertical, the opposite blade should be almost horizontal. Now twist your control wrist back to bring your knuckles toward you as if giving the gas to a motorcycle. Bring your wrist far enough back so that the blades switch positions, with the control blade now being almost horizontal and the non-control blade vertical. Try it again, but this time bend your elbow to raise your forearm as you twist your wrist. Don't juggle the shaft around in your hands to change the blade angle. Hold onto the shaft securely with your control hand. Let your wrist and forearm do the

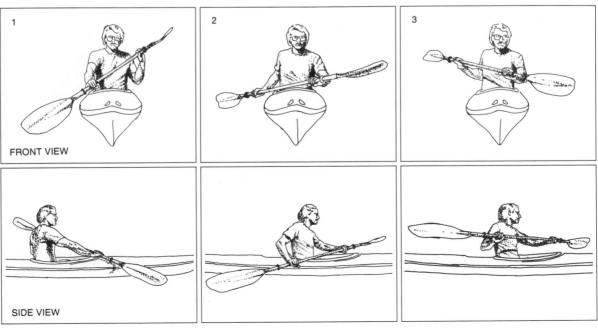

1

FRONT VIEW

2

3

SIDE VIEW

angle changing. Practice until you are confident about being able to present a vertical blade to the water on either side. See if you can do it with your eyes closed, using only the feel of your control hand.

For some reason it often seems easier to make your first stroke on the control side. So put the control-side blade in first and go through the same hand and arm motions as you did with the non-feathered paddle. On the control side the stroke is exactly the same until you lift the blade from the water. It is here that you begin to raise the forearm and twist the wrist back. This will bring the non-control blade vertical, down, forward, and ready for the stroke on the other side.

Put the non-control blade in and begin pulling yourself toward it while straightening the opposite arm. At this point you can ease (but not reposition) your control-hand grip, palm facing down and forward, with fingers relaxed and wrist fairly straight.

Lift the blade out when it is opposite your hips. As you continue lifting begin to twist the control wrist forward, while lowering and extending the forearm. This will bring the control blade vertical, down, and forward. The

cycle is complete and you are ready to start the stroke again on the control side.

Don't get discouraged if your beginning strokes end in disaster. Paddling takes a tremendous amount of practice before you can attain a good fluid stroke. Common problems at this stage are: not using the full blade, leaning forward to extend your reach, too tight a grip, bringing the upper hand across the centerline, and continuing the stroke beyond the hip. With all the wrist twisting and relaxing of fingers there is the possibility of losing orientation between the control hand and the blade. Occasionally check your grip to be sure.

Don't think yourself a weakling because you feel beat after paddling short distances. It's not you. It's because you've only been using the relatively small muscles in your arms. No paddler is strong enough to go any distance on their arms alone. Next you'll be adding the pushing of the opposing arm, and then the more powerful muscles of your abdomen, back, shoulder, and legs. But for now, just work on the arms and the pattern of the blade in the water.

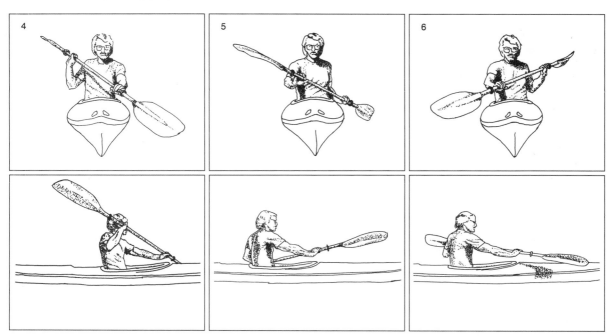

Push/Pull

By now you've probably managed to make the boat move by using your arms to pull it through the water. It worked, but it was hard work. That's because you were using only one arm for the job, while letting the other just guide the paddle without putting in its fair share. Well the free ride is over for that "other" non-pulling arm, now you'll use it to provide a pushing force to complement the pulling arm's effort. By adding this extra power from your upper arm you'll immediately find a great strain has been taken off your pulling wrist and that paddling has become a whole lot easier.

The additional pushing motion is like using two hands to turn a wheel instead of one; or, if you prefer a more literal image, it might help to think of the paddle as a lever.

Envision at the start of each stroke that the blade is being inserted into something solid and that you are pulling the boat toward it. With this action you are using the paddle as a lever. Unfortunately it is a very inefficient one, but with the addition of some pushing from the upper arm, leverage is improved markedly.

Now envision a new and more complex lever. Like all levers, it needs a pivot point, a fulcrum—your pulling hand. As before, you are trying to move an immovable blade through the water to pry the boat forward. But now, the motive forces will come from both the pulling and pushing arms.

What makes this lever complex is that your pulling hand becomes a moveable fulcrum. As it hauls the boat toward the blade it is also acting as a pivot point for the shaft, which is being pushed forward by the upper arm. The result is a combined increase in power from the hauling of the pulling arm and the leveraged prying of the pushing arm.

However you understand it, both arms are now sharing the work. The balance isn't even, with about 65 percent of the force coming from pulling and 35 percent from pushing; but it's more than enough for you to be able to notice a tremendous difference in performance.

The pushing begins as soon as you start the stroke with your lower pulling arm. The two hands move in opposite directions but at similar speeds. The pushing force increases through the middle of the stroke, about where your knee

passes the blade. At this point both arms are equally extended and maximum pushing power is being applied. The arms continue the stroke with reduced force until the lower pulling hand is at the end of its stroke and the upper pushing arm almost at the limit of its reach. The total motion of the pushing arm is like a slow, forward punch coming from your shoulder toward the centerline at the bow.

There is a tendency to get overenthusiastic about pushing. Some paddlers may complete the push way before the pull has finished, or apply maximum push before the pull has even started. Enthusiasm may also bring an overabundance of power. While learning keep your cadence (pace) down, use gentle pressure so you can feel the pushing, pulling, and where the two change places.

Bringing the pushing hand above eye level, dropping it near the end of the stroke, crossing the boat's centerline, or holding the shaft too close to your chest will all limit the success of your pushing. Don't develop a death grip with your upper hand. Keep fingers relaxed and slightly open, with the palm taking most of the pressure.

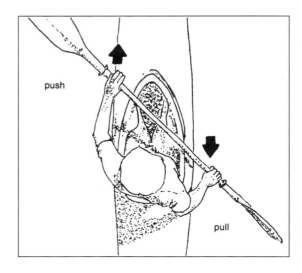

Body Twist

Put your back into it! And well you should, because the more (and larger) muscles you can enlist to help, the easier the job becomes.

Instead of sawing back and forth with your arm when using a handsaw, you probably figured out that the more efficient way was to move your shoulders and put the muscle and momentum of your body into it. You got further faster and with less effort. It's the same with paddling. To get the full range of motion and the benefit of the muscles in your abdomen, back, and shoulders you will have to sit upright without slouching or leaning back. And even more than before, you'll need to be well braced in the kayak. Your feet, legs, and hips should be as one with the boat, while leaving you free to move from the waist up.

The stroke begins as before with one arm extended ahead, and the other bent and close to your body. To this you add body twist by swinging the shoulder of the extended arm forward. No need to go into contortions, just a comfortable rotation of the torso without straining the waist or back.

This position sets your body to recoil with full power. It also increases your reach so you can put the blade in farther forward, extending the useful length of your stroke.

The releasing of the collective body power that rotates the shoulder begins when the pulling arm starts the stroke. This release has a multiple effect: As your pulling shoulder comes back, the shoulder on the pushing side is going forward. Both the pulling and pushing components of your stroke are being augmented.

During the stroke's maximum power phase almost all the paddling force is coming from your torso, and the least from your pushing arm, with the rest supplied by the pulling arm. The body's motion is not a jerk or a snatch, but a smooth uncoiling of a powerful spring. By keeping your arms slightly bent and away from your chest you will get the full use of this power. You can also help, and it might even come naturally, by pressing the foot brace on the stroke side. This is a reflexive action that helps to push the kayak forward. As you take a stroke on the right side, press on the right foot brace; stroke on the left, press on the left.

When the blade is withdrawn at the end of the stroke both the pulling and pushing shoulders will have followed through an almost-90-degree swing. The pulling shoulder is now pointing back, and the pushing shoulder is now close to the same angle as your pulling shoulder was at the beginning of the stroke. This sets you up to start on the other side.

An interesting experiment is to restrict arm motion by keeping both arms locked, using only body twist to do the work. You might surprise yourself with your own power. You can also play at seeing how far you can exaggerate the twisting. Try accelerating from a dead stop to see which muscles are really being used. You should feel it in your abdomen, as if you were doing sit ups, and in your legs from pushing on the foot braces. At first your legs and abdomen may ache, but as muscles strengthen, this will go away. The more you incorporate body twist into your stroke, the more the soreness of unused muscles leaves the arms for the shoulders and abdomen. Eventually even this gives way to a stroke that feels effortless.

While body twist should be used as much as possible, you need not go to extremes. For most paddling only gentle forces need be applied with small amounts of rotation. Only when confronted with strong winds or currents will you need to really coil up and unwind the body's full power.

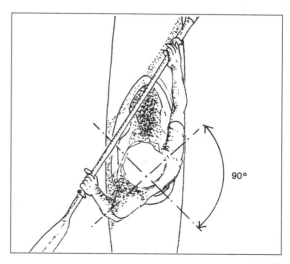

90°

PADDLING

The Complete Stroke

There are very few absolutes when it comes to paddling; what standards there are have been presented. Take them only as a foundation, something from which you can build a style that is uniquely your own. From here on you should strive to develop a stroke that is both powerful and comfortable.

To do this you will have to relinquish the idea of separate wrist, arm, and body motions. Your goal is a more fluid stroke. The best way to achieve this is through practice; and that means constant practice, for long stretches at a time. While training try not to think the stroke through. Let it happen on its own, and when you feel it's right, put your brain in gear to watch what you're doing. Don't be discouraged if it takes time. And every once and a while go back to working on the fundamental components, just to make sure you aren't sacrificing a small part for the sake of the total package.

Dos and Don'ts

Here is a quick review of things you should *do* while practicing:

- Keep the power blade fully immersed and perpendicular to the water.
- Keep a constant alignment of the controlling hand to the nearest blade.
- Center your grip on the shaft and keep it loose.
- Sit upright with your head steady and eyes on the horizon.
- Hold the shaft away from your chest with elbows slightly bent.
- Place the blade as far ahead as possible at the beginning of the stroke without bending forward at the waist.
- Bring your shoulder forward to increase your reach.
- Put the blade in close to the boat and cleanly so there is no splash.
- Use the palm of the upper hand to push, guided by slightly opened fingers.

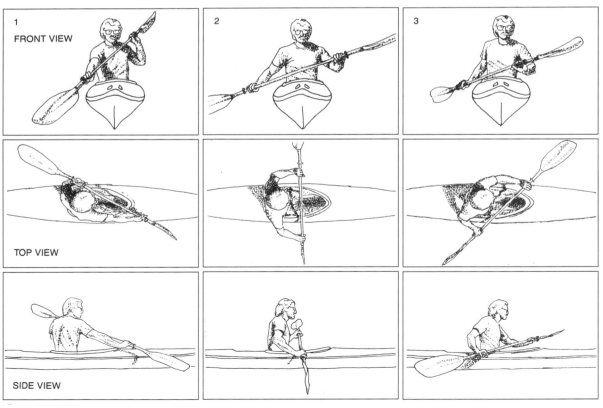

1   FRONT VIEW   2   3

TOP VIEW

SIDE VIEW

- Maintain as shallow a shaft angle as practical.
- Pull and push with a steady, even pressure that favors the pulling side.
- Get the majority of your power from the torso, then the pulling arm, and least of all from the pushing arm.
- Twist your torso and rotate your shoulders to pull one arm back while driving the other arm forward.
- Push against the foot brace on the pulling side.
- Apply maximum power in mid-stroke, usually as knees are passing the blade.
- Slice the blade up and out cleanly when your hip passes it.
- Avoid unnecessary force.

- Allow the pushing hand to go above eye level or across the centerline of the boat.
- Keep too tight a grip on the shaft.
- Juggle your grip to change the blade's angle to the water.
- Paddle using only your arms.
- Keep the upper blade high in the air to catch wind and drip water on you.
- Apply power before the blade is fully immersed.
- Continue the stroke far beyond your hips.
- Lean back and forth, or rock side to side, as you paddle.
- Take the blade out too early, losing power—or too late, creating drag.

Here is a quick review of things you *don't* want to do while practicing:

- Slouch or lean back in the seat.
- Hold arms close to the chest.

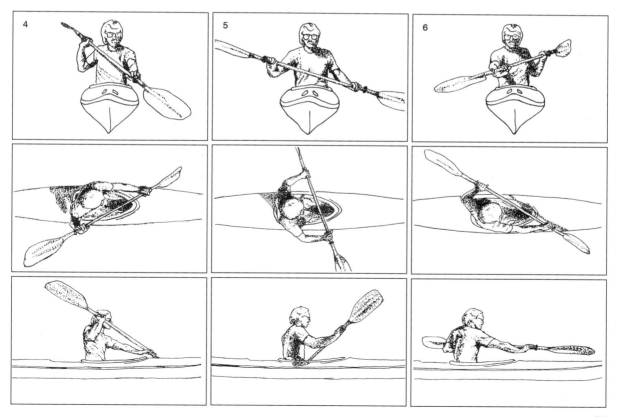

Stopping and Backing

Although forward progress is always desirable, there are times when a hasty retreat will become prudent if not damn near life saving. Besides general maneuvering, backing can be used as a holding action when caught in a current, give you time to contemplate your next move, or keep you in position on a breaking wave. But before going backward it is worthwhile to first look into the techniques of stopping.

A kayak's maximum speed is not likely to exceed 5 mph, yet its momentum can come as quite a shock when you attempt to stop. Since a lot of effort and balance are needed to do this, it will be best not to try with one Herculean stroke.

When you decide to stop, hold the shaft low and near your body with elbows tucked in. Have the blade slightly behind your hip and maintain a vertical, or slightly forward-leaning, blade angle. Immerse one blade for a second or two, and then the other. Your arms should stay flexible, pushing forward slightly, while your body twists to absorb most of the energy. Do not change your grip on the shaft in order to turn the power face frontward. In doing so you risk losing your hand's orientation to the blade; the resistance of the back of the blade will be more than enough. To stop in a straight line, try to provide an even braking force by not keeping one blade in longer than the other. Three or four quick jabs on alternate sides should do it.

The forces absorbed with body twist in stopping will be reinvested in the backstroke, for its power comes almost exclusively from the torso. Position yourself in the boat so you are sitting upright or leaning back slightly, making sure that your seat and lower back are locked in place to take the transmitted drive. As with stopping, your grip is never changed and only the back side of the blade is used.

The starting position is with the body fully rotated and the paddle held almost parallel to the side of the boat. The blade is put in about two feet behind the hips, with arms and elbows close to the body. You then unwind (rotate) forward bringing your arms and the paddle with you while leaning back to put your weight behind the stroke. Some pushing with the palm, keeping fingers relaxed, may be incorpo-

rated to help direct the blade. Maximum power is utilized as the hips pass, and the blade is lifted up and out as the knees pass.

To get the most power from your backstroke hold the shaft so that the full back of the blade touches the water as it enters. The paddle is kept as vertical and parallel to the side of the boat as possible throughout the stroke, with power being exerted down and forward. A less powerful stroke, but with more steering ability, can be had by slipping the blade in edge first and making the stroke a broad sweep. Power here is exerted out and forward. The typical backing stroke will be somewhere between these two extremes, varying to hold the desired course.

The faster you paddle, the harder it is to steer. So paddle slowly, making adjustments in your stroke as you go. Balance may also prove difficult. Looking over one shoulder and then the other is sure to disorient you. So pick one and keep your eyes on a fixed point of reference. If any distances are involved, you need only give an occasional look over that one shoulder, or use a reference point off your bow to guide you.

STOPPING

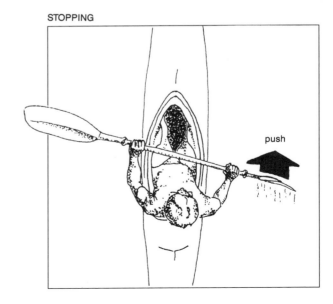

push

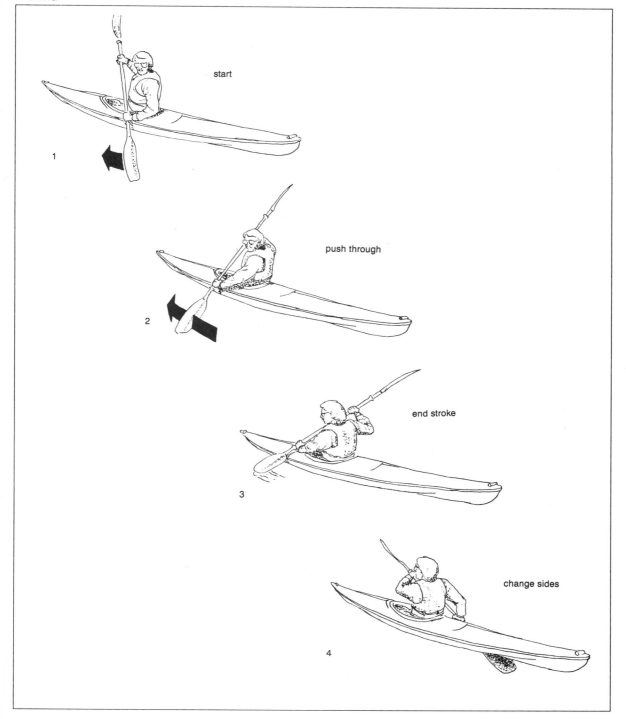

start

1

push through

2

end stroke

3

change sides

4

Fine Points

Feathered vs. non-feathered: You need no other reason to choose one over the other than a simple "It works for me". Even so, it does seem a paradox. How can one be just as good as the other if they are so different? Maybe a little bit of history will clarify the matter.

For centuries the Eskimos used relatively long paddles with narrow blades. These were perfect for traveling great distances at a constant speed, easy to control in high winds, and unequaled for the job they were intended to do.

Then, around the middle of the 1800s, the kayak was introduced to "civilization" and put to uses other than what it was originally designed for. There was no longer a need to paddle twenty miles at a clip or sneak up on a walrus. The evolving turn-of-the-century sportsman was more interested in increasing the power of his stroke for quicker spurts than in long-range endurance, so he devised a completely different paddle. This new paddle used bigger blades for more power, and was shorter for a more rapid stroke. It also did the job it was intended to do, except for one problem. When paddling into a headwind it took a lot of effort to push that big blade through the air on the return stroke. To alleviate this someone set the blades at opposing angles (feathered). Now the returning blade went through the air horizontally, so its size was no longer a problem. A side benefit for some was that, although the motion was more complex, it seemed less choppy and more harmonious than the old style. So feathering was born, and has stayed on. Just for the record, here's what the "experts" say about each.

Non-feathered: The main advantage to this style is that it is supposedly easier on the wrists and forearms, although poor technique has been known to negate this advantage. The drawback is that with larger modern blades there is more resistance when going into the wind; but paddle control is easier when the wind is from the side. The combined arm and upper body movements are simpler, but seem awkward to some. It is claimed to work best with a flatter stroke using long paddles with smaller blades, making it suited for wide, heavy, slower boats.

Feathered: It is believed that there is a mechanical advantage to feathering because it allows more powerful upper body rotation, and that it is better suited to a more vertical stroke on narrow, light, fast boats. The wrist and forearm of the control hand are susceptible to strains, but this can be avoided through proper technique. There is less resistance while paddling into a headwind, although strong side winds make the paddle harder to control. The wrist, arm, and upper body movements take more time to get used to, but feel quite natural once mastered. It is claimed to work best with shorter paddles and larger blades.

So you see there is no answer. Try both. Give each a fair chance. Pick one, and then stick with it. Practice good technique for whichever you choose. Do warm-up exercises before paddling.

You should always warm up before paddling. This need not be a half-hour workout, just a few stretching exercises. Try toe touching, arm circles, and head and shoulder rotations.

No matter which style you choose be aware of the position of your wrists in relation to your forearms. Try to maintain a neutral wrist position, which is the relationship that your forearm, wrist, and hand fall into when they hang at your side. In this neutral position the wrist is relaxed, and there is minimal wear and strain on the interconnecting tendons. One of the best ways of assuring this is to keep a loose, open grip on the shaft. This means pushing primarily with the palm near the thumb and forefinger while keeping fingers relaxed, and beginning the pulling stroke with the last three fingers extended and the shaft cradled between thumb and forefinger. In addition, a loose grip also improves blood circulation and hand warmth, and reduces the likelihood of tendonitis or blisters. Keeping your hands dry can also prevent blisters. Do this with drip rings and by paddling with a low shaft angle.

The forward stroke is remarkably variable. Strokes where the paddle is nearly vertical, passing close to the hull and parallel to the centerline have the most propulsive and the least turning or supporting effect. This is your power or racing stroke. It provides maximum drive, but offers little lateral support or steering moment.

Strokes where the paddle is held at a low angle, so it makes a broad sweeping arc, have less propulsive but more turning or supporting effect. This is your control stroke. It provides plenty of lateral support and steering moment, but offers less drive. Between these extremes you will be able to find strokes that propel the kayak at a good speed, for long distances, with adequate steering control through a wide variety of sea conditions.

Besides the basic propulsion strokes, you will learn others that can turn the kayak or aid in stability. None is a separate entity, and all should be integrated to link together. This linking of strokes provides an economy of effort that allows you to exert less power to achieve the same results with fewer strokes. Keep this in mind as your repertoire of maneuvers increases.

Finding that the boat won't go straight? Try paddling slowly and thoughtfully at first. Many novices paddle too vigorously at the expense of good control. They wind up being unable to hold a course, and wander all over the place. The more force you put into a stroke the more perfect it must be. So go easy. And don't rush it either. A reasonable cruising cadence (pace) is about three seconds for a complete cycle. But this can vary according to the type of paddle and conditions.

The inability to keep a straight course can also come from uneven leverage on the shaft. Everyone has one arm that is stronger than the other. If this is not kept in check you'll have a more powerful stroke on your stronger side. Another cause is that your grip might shift off center. To prevent this use tape to mark reference points on the shaft.

Don't rock the boat. Literally. Don't lean forward when you put the blade in, and don't lean back when you take it out. The bobbing motion created by this back-and-forth leaning wastes energy and slows down the kayak. Side-to-side rocking comes from shifting your weight and leaning over with each stroke. This too is wasteful.

In the beginning it's alright and probably necessary to watch each blade's path through the water, your hands on the shaft, and all the rest that is new. Continue doing this only until you've got a sense for where each blade is during the cycle. From then on start keeping your head up. Find a landmark in the distance and go for it. This will help you steer with small corrective adjustments in your stroke and learn to understand what you are doing by feel, not sight.

Don't forget to breathe. If you concentrate too hard you may not breathe at regular intervals and only make it a short distance before getting out of breath. Try to keep your head up, inhale at the beginning of a stroke on one side and exhale at the beginning of a stroke on the other. Develop a rhythm. Relaxation during the stoke is also important. If you're tense and putting out all the time you'll collapse after a mile. Ease up, and take a split second off in the transition period between strokes.

Your blade is not a windmill making great arcs in the sky. Seen from the side the tip of each blade makes an oval, not a circular, path during its cycle.

You might find that the "perfect" stroke as described here may not work for you. And that's OK. Everyone has an individual style that incorporates at least some of these elements. Do what you can to get close, while at the same time working within the limitations of your own body. You are not a machine.

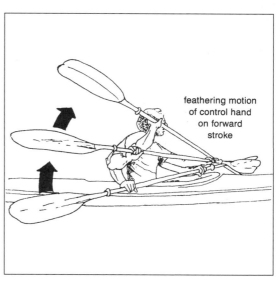

feathering motion of control hand on forward stroke

MANEUVERING

Forward Sweep

The forward sweep is the most fundamental of all turning strokes and seems to come almost intuitively. It's obvious: Make a broad sweeping stroke on one side and the boat turns to the other. Use it while standing still to turn the boat within a small area, or when underway as a variation of the forward stroke for course alterations.

The forces involved are similar to those of the forward stroke. You put the blade in the water near the bow and from then on consider it as being inserted into something solid. The motion is a swing through almost half a circle. For the first part of the sweep you are pushing the bow away from the blade. During the middle part a forward motion is imparted to the boat. And for the last part of the sweep you are pulling the stern toward the blade.

To begin, hold the paddle in front of you. Then, without changing your grip on the shaft, move your arms and the paddle out toward the side you will sweep on. The sweeping arm should be almost straight and the hand of the other arm resting near your body over the boat's centerline.

In this extended position, rotate your shoulders to bring the blade as far forward as possible. Put the blade in so it is fully immersed, maintain an open grip, and lean slightly forward. Holding the paddle shaft as close to horizontal as you can, use the twisting of your body to swing it in a low broad sweep. To help move the boat, press forward on the sweeping side with your foot, and to the side with your knee or thigh. Throughout most of the stroke think of your arms, shoulders, and the paddle shaft as being locked in place and pivoting around the axis of your body, the spine. Power should come almost exclusively from the unwinding of your body, with some arm pull to help guide the blade. Only toward the last third of the stroke will the other arm push out a little to help pull your hips to the paddle and bring the stroke through its full arc.

Just before the blade reaches the boat bend the elbow of the sweeping arm to pull it up. Try not to turn the blade's power face up at the end of the stroke. This only lifts water and wastes energy.

A sweep stroke while underway works a little differently because the water moving past the boat begins to carry the blade aft as soon as it is put in. The beginning part of the sweep has some turning and propulsive components, the middle part some turning and a lot of propulsive. The last part of the sweep has a great amount of turning and almost no propulsive component. Keep these factors in mind as you adjust your course.

Since sea kayaks are designed to travel in a straight line it takes a lot of work to turn them. But don't overdo it. If you are dragging the blade through the water with a lot of fuss and turbulence, ease up. All you are doing is aerating the ocean, causing your blade to slip rather than push or pull the boat around. The best way to improve the boat's turning ability is to reduce its underwater length by leaning it on its side. Tilt the boat only slightly towards the side of the stroke by pushing up with the knee on the opposite side from the sweep.

Another way to improve turning ability is by extending the paddle out even farther. To do this place the sweeping hand near the center of the shaft and the other hand by the throat of the non-sweeping blade. This makes a longer lever arm, but is not without some risks. By moving your hands you lose orientation to the blades, which may leave you momentarily vulnerable as you get reorganized for another stroke. Try to maintain the same grip for almost all maneuvers.

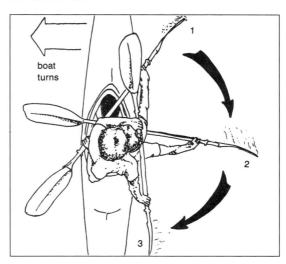

Reverse Sweep

Reverse sweeps are very useful when sudden changes of direction and braking are needed. There's not a whole lot of difference between the forward and reverse sweep. But what there is, is important.

The main difference is power from the body. What you give up for power is stability. Because your body is centered directly over the paddle at the beginning of the stroke your center of gravity is higher and you are not as solidly rooted as with other strokes.

Most everything else is very much like a forward sweep done backwards. The hand, arm, body, and paddle positions are the same. Blade positions, too, do not change, although the stroke is made using the back not the power face. Sitting upright you rotate your body and reach as far back as you can, keeping the sweeping arm straight. Hold the paddle shaft as close to horizontal as possible and swing forward in a low broad arc while pushing yourself back with the foot on the sweep side. Apply greatest force in the more effective first third of the sweep. Almost all power should come from the twisting of the body, with some pushing of the sweeping arm for guidance and pulling from the other arm near the end of the stroke. At the completion of the arc withdraw the blade sharply before hitting the side of the kayak. You might also want to lean forward at the end, adding a little extra power to what would normally be a weak position.

While standing still you can spin the boat within its own length by alternating forward and reverse sweeps on opposite sides. While moving, the first third of the reverse stroke is a powerful way to steer. And when combined with other strokes, like the stern rudder or low brace, it becomes part of the most powerful steering combination available.

Both the forward and reverse sweeps, like the forward paddling stroke, lend themselves to linking together with other strokes. Go for smooth transitions and economy of motion.

Stern Rudder Stroke

The stern rudder is not a stroke in the strictest sense of the word. You do not place the blade in the water and actively push or pull the kayak around it. It is more of a passive action, where the flow of water past the kayak is deflected to induce a turn. The result is precise control without losing too much boat speed. It can be used for fine course corrections while paddling, in tight spots where wide sweeping strokes won't work, or for sharp turns when considerable momentum has been built up as in going downwind or sliding down the face of a wave.

To steer with the stern rudder, rotate your body and trail the blade on the side you wish to turn to as if setting up for a reverse sweep. The arm farthest back, which takes the force of the steering, is kept almost straight, with the other bent and held near the body. The blade is fully immersed, vertical in relation to the water, and set off at a shallow angle from the boat, about a foot away, with the back of the blade facing out. By simply holding the blade you will immediately cause the boat to turn to the side that the blade is on. By adding a pushing resistance, not a sweep, you can tighten the turn.

More versatility can be had by holding the paddle away from, and nearly parallel to, the boat. In this way you can make turns in either direction. Slightly less powerful turns can be made as before by pushing the blade away from the boat. Turns toward the opposite direction, but with considerably less range and dramatic results, can be made by pulling the blade towards the boat.

In any situation, too much pushing or pulling resistance will ultimately slow the boat. This affects turning ability because the power of the stern rudder is directly related to the speed of the boat through the water. The faster the kayak is going, the more responsive it is to rudder motion.

There are refinements that can be added to the stern rudder to improve its utility and effectiveness. By rolling the wrist you can change the angle of the blade to the water and improve its worth as a deflecting vane. Just tilt the top of the blade towards the direction you would like to turn. This can be used on its own with the blade held in one position for ultra-delicate course changes, or in conjunction with a pushed or pulled stern rudder to augment the effect. Another refinement is to use the paddle as a tiller. The rear hand stays in place and the forward hand pushes or pulls the shaft to act like the tiller on a sailboat. In theory the "tiller" acts as a lever to put greater effort into a turn.

The stern rudder is rarely used on its own. Most often it is part of a series of strokes. For instance it works well when added on at the end of a forward stroke, which is convenient because you have to be moving at a fair clip to use the rudder anyway. It also links up with, or converts easily into, the beginnings of a reverse sweep or a low brace. Try combinations so you can flow from one stroke to another, making a continuous maneuver out of separate elements.

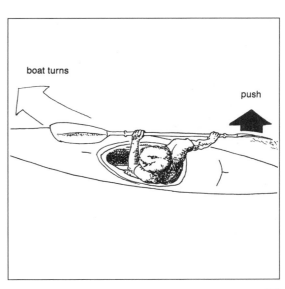

boat turns

push

MANEUVERING

Rudders

The rudder is a relatively recent advancement in marine engineering and was a major technological breakthrough for its time. Centuries before recorded history vessels were steered by a stern rudder stroke from a paddle, which was later marginally improved upon by lashing the paddle to one side of a pointed stern to allow for rotation. By about 1200 A.D., this steering board (from which we got the word starboard) arrangement was replaced by the incredibly efficient rudder. For larger vessels there is no better steering device. For kayaks they are not quite the panacea they might seem.

Rudders for kayaks are a very recent development and have proven to be both a boon and a boondoggle. Today most sea kayaks either come with rudders, offer them as accessories, or can be adapted by after-market products. The contemporary rudder is tough, dependable, and ideally suited to resolving problems of weathercocking.

Almost all kayaks, regardless of manufacturers' claims, swing around in response to the wind. When underway most boats want to weathercock so their bow points into the wind, which is the safer of the two possibilities. The drawback is that this makes holding a course across or away from the wind difficult and tiring. By using a rudder this natural turning tendency can be counteracted, letting you put all your energy into propulsion rather than steering. This is where the rudder is a boon.

The boondoggle part comes from what you give up for the convenience. Probably the greatest sacrifice is the loss of firm foot bracing. Some rudder systems lock the foot pedals in place when not in use, but once engaged the pedals move and solid bracing is gone. Other systems can not be locked in place at all. In these cases your only option is to brace your heels on the bottom of the boat and push against them.

Almost all rudders are foot controlled. Press on the right foot pedal, the rudder and boat turn to the right. Left foot, left turn. Since rudders are so efficient only a small angle is needed to produce a turn. Compared to the stern rudder stroke they produce hardly any drag, which means that they are less likely to slow the boat down and require a minimum amount of effort to intiate a turn.

Because of its turning power the rudder need only be used sparingly. There is no reason to throw it way over to one side in order to start a turn. Make minor corrections, watch the bow swing, and before it is pointing where you would like, bring the rudder back to center. Don't wait until you need to make large corrections. Catch it with subtle rudder movements. When in waves or a steady wind from one direction, paddle with the rudder set at a constant minimal angle. Don't try to adjust your course for every wave that yaws you one way and then the next. You'll impede the boat's progress and eventually drive yourself nuts. If you can keep within 10 degrees of a course, you're doing just fine.

Like any other mechanical contrivance rudders are susceptible to breakage, usually when you need them most. They are particularly vulnerable in the surf, around rocks, or in shallows. Undeniably, rudders are wonderful things; but don't get too dependent on them. If your boat is not too sensitive to the wind, rely on your paddling ability first; a rudder can never replace this. If your boat needs a rudder, use it as a way of making life easier. Keep it cocked up until needed and then use it intelligently.

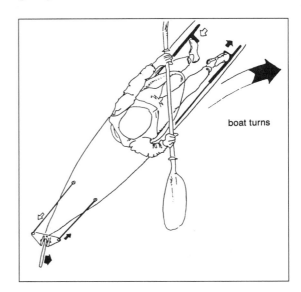

boat turns

Draw Stroke

The kayak is one of the few vessels that can be made to travel sideways with any sort of control. This comes in very handy for maneuvering around obstacles, rafting up with others, and positioning yourself to aid in a rescue.

When moving to the side you should use a draw stroke for strong bursts of power to cover short distances in a hurry. It is simple and direct. You place your blade in the water and then haul the boat towards it.

To set up for the stroke hold the paddle in the forward paddling grip and turn your body to the side. Reach out and bring the shaft almost to vertical with the power face of the blade inward. Put the blade in two to three feet from the boat directly opposite your hips, and immersed to the throat. The lower arm will be straight and the upper one bent about 90 degrees.

The main action of the stroke is a pull from the lower arm at about waist height. Most of the power comes from this arm, with only a small amount from the upper arm adding some pushing motion. As you pull, the boat will have a tendency to lean into the stroke, hindering its ability to slip over the water. With a gentle stroke this will be of no concern but, if you're putting some oomph into it, you'll want to level the boat by pushing up with your knee on the stroke side.

Do not let the blade get under the kayak. When about a foot from the blade, twist your lower wrist so the shaft rotates 90 degrees, causing the power face to look aft. Set like this the blade can be knifed back through the water to the set-up position where you can straighten your wrist and draw it back in again. To end the stroke, or for those having trouble changing blade angle, the blade can be lifted clear of the water. At the end of the draw bring your upper arm forward and your lower arm back. This will slice the blade up and out. From here you can proceed into something else (like a reverse sweep), or begin the draw once again.

During successive strokes you'll find that one end of the boat advances more quickly than the other. To correct this, direct your pull towards the end that is lagging behind.

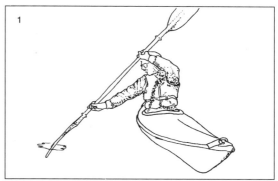

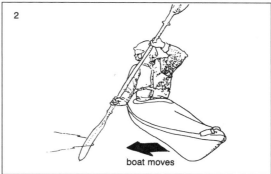

boat moves

Sculling Draw

The sculling draw stroke provides a constant pull moving the kayak sideways. It won't give you the draw stroke's bursts of power and requires a bit of finesse, but because there is no recovery phase you get an uninterrupted motion that is easier to control with less chance of being caught off balance.

Sculling is a continuous movement rather than a single stroke. By slicing an angled blade through the water you create an action which is very similar to that of a slow-moving propeller. The resultant force can be used to pull you, and the boat you are attached to, sideways through the water.

To get a feel for this force try an experiment. Stand in hip-deep water, hold the paddle vertical, and move it back and forth through the water. If the blade is held broadside to the motion, as it would be when you are paddling, you'll feel yourself being forced forward and back. But if the blade is held at an angle to the motion, you'll feel a pulling or pushing force to the side. Play at this long enough and you'll notice that the direction of the lateral force relates to the blade's angle, which is determined by its leading edge. If the edge closest to you is leading, the paddle will be pushing inward. If the edge farthest from you is leading the motion, the paddle will pull away. This pulling effect is the basic principle of sculling.

The starting position is almost the same as for the draw stroke: normal forward paddling grip, body turned, shaft almost vertical, blade well immersed with power face in and placed about two feet from the boat. The lower arm will provide all the power and is kept bent throughout the stroke. The upper arm is held high and arched slightly, providing a pivot for the shaft. In this position your upper wrist might seem awkwardly twisted, but do not change over to an underhand grip. You may not have the time or presence of mind to change back in an emergency.

Turn the blade so that one of its edges is angled away from the boat approximately 30 degrees from centerline. The paddle's motion will be in the direction of this edge and will cause the blade to pull away from the boat. By resisting this you transmit the pull to the kayak and follow the blade sideways.

The angled blade, power face first, is sliced forward about four feet. At the end of its travel the blade angle is reversed and the paddle sliced aft, power face first, for the same distance. Blade-angle switching is done as in feathering, with a quick twist of the control hand's wrist. The angle is always directed by the control hand. This is so regardless of whether the control hand is in the upper or lower position. The cycle should be smooth and feel continuous with no stopping where blade angles switch.

Seen from above the paddle is pulled back and forth in a path that is parallel to the boat's centerline at a constant distance from the hull. As with the draw stroke, you may find that one end of the boat is advancing more quickly than the other. To correct this, direct your pull towards the end that is lagging behind. You may also need to push up with the knee on the sculling side to keep the boat from leaning into the stroke and hindering side slip.

A tricky adaptation of the sculling draw is to do it backward. Go through the movements in the same way, except use the back of the blade with the edge closest to you leading the motion. This will push the paddle towards the boat, instead of pulling it away. Use this to get an extra touch of control without having to change sculling sides.

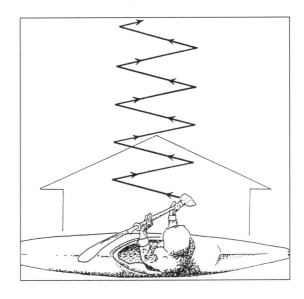

Linking Strokes

Every dance instructor knows that you can learn all the steps in the world but if you can't put them together, it ain't dancin' and you might as well not even bother going out on the floor. Dancing over the waves is the same. You can learn all the strokes but if you can't link them together, it ain't kayaking and you had better think twice about heading off into the sunset.

Besides the basic propulsion and maneuvering strokes, there are others that enhance stability. Each one is unique, with traits and nuances that have to be learned on their own. Yet none of these strokes is intended to exist as a separate entity; they have to be integrated, or linked, together.

The objective of this linking is an improved economy of effort, allowing you to exert less power to achieve the same results with fewer strokes. That's the goal. But even before getting to that point you can begin to benefit from stroke linking right now, during the learning process. Not only are most strokes intended to work together, they are also interrelated in technique. For instance the stern rudder, reverse sweep, and sweeping low brace all have common elements. If you learn one, that information can be transposed to the others. By linking the strokes, using them together, you find these common elements and expand your capabilities.

As your repertoire of strokes increases, experiment with paddling through trial and, just as importantly, error. Try combinations; see how they join up. Work towards flowing from one stroke to another, making a continuous maneuver out of separate elements. Go for smooth transitions and minimal amounts of extraneous motion. At the same time try to develop what has been called "paddle awareness," or knowing where your paddle and blades are at all times without having to look at them. This requires that you maintain a constant and uniform grip with your control hand. The closer it comes to being instinctive the more you will enjoy paddling and feel at home in your kayak. You can't react properly without this awareness. Very often there are situations when there is no time to stop and figure out what's going on. You'll only be able to react.

Some Drills

To give you some idea of what is meant by linked strokes, and at the same time offer practice routines, here are a few ways in which the strokes you have learned so far can be joined together.

Sweeps. Paddle forward; on one right-hand stroke convert to a forward sweep; then to a reverse sweep on the left side; the boat will turn sharply to the left; leave the blade in after the reverse sweep and begin in the new direction with a forward stroke.

Sideways. Do two draw strokes; at the end of the last draw change to a sculling stroke; at the end of a forward slice convert to a forward stroke; gather speed and position the blade for a lateral shift.

Backward. Paddle backward over a twisting course; make a sudden stop; turn in place using forward and reverse sweeps so you are pointing in the opposite direction; paddle back through the same twisting course.

As you can imagine, the variations are endless. Make up your own slalom course with strokes for going forward, backward, sideways, turning, and later on, bracing. Vary from one side to the next and practice these combinations as you would individual strokes.

BRACING

Principles

Sea kayaking isn't yachting, it's a water sport, and every once in a while you can expect to get wet or maybe even knocked over. But that's all part of it, as are the skills of staying upright and knowing how to keep going when it gets rough. These skills are basic to the sport and are encompassed in a group of strokes known as braces.

Bracing strokes can be used for recovery or support. A recovery stroke brings you upright from an unstable position, while a support stroke holds you in a stable one. Combine them with good balance, a strong forward stroke, and the ability to maneuver, and you and your kayak become an impressively seaworthy unit.

The feeling of self-assurance that comes with dependable bracing is fantastic and it's a big part of the fascination most paddlers have with the sport. But you'll never know this until your bracing skills become something you can trust implicitly. Once attained, your whole approach to sea kayaking will be different. A lot of the worries and most of the fears will be gone, replaced with a new sense of confidence. You'll be able to extend your limits and finally begin to evolve a style that is uniquely yours.

At the start, bracing seems a little unnatural. Normally when you feel yourself losing balance and there is nothing to stop you, you lean the other way. In a kayak where there is obviously nothing that is going to keep you from going over, it is understandable that you would also try to do the same thing. But this is just what you should not do. The proper response is to reach out to the one thing that seems least likely to be of any help: The water.

At 800 times the density of air and virtually incompressible, water can feel very solid indeed. Remember those painful belly-flop dives when you were a kid and how unyielding the water felt? Well, one bracing stroke uses that very same principle.

And remember sticking your hand out the car window to play airplane? With your hand level you'd fly along; but if you angled it up you'd take off. Now think of something as dense as water and "flying" something even bigger than your hand through it like a paddle blade. It doesn't take a rocket scientist to figure out that a moving blade just might be able to

support quite a lot of weight, keeping you and your kayak from going over.

Without getting into the fluid dynamics of stalled foils, it's sufficient to understand that if the forward edge of a blade in motion is kept at a climbing angle, you'll get lift. This works whether the blade is being moved or held stationary with the water moving. It also works below the surface as well as on it. And the larger the blade, or the faster the water, the more lift you get.

Try standing in hip-deep water and swinging the paddle around so it skims the surface. Make it plane like a water ski and really lean on it to see how much weight it can take. You'll be surprised.

A more practical application is to incorporate that lift into your forward paddling stroke by angling the blade back slightly. This gives both propulsion and support, and is a very subtle example of linking strokes.

When practicing, gradually increase the pressure you put on the paddle until you've proven to yourself that bracing works. From then on, don't hold back; be willing to commit yourself to your skill. Even though you may capsize a few times, in the end you will have to depend on your ability to brace, so keep trying. A solid paddle float may be helpful while learning and a good fit with your boat is a must.

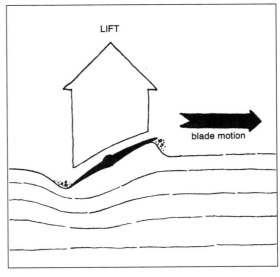

Slap Brace

A slap brace is a recovery stroke, something you do when you're caught off balance just as you're saying "oops." It's a way of catching yourself before going over.

The premise is simple, and almost instinctive. You only have to believe that, for a second or two, water can be solid. Once you accept this, it's like putting your hand out to stop a fall. Only here the paddle becomes your hand, or at least an extension of it. When you feel yourself going over you reach to that side and slap the back of the blade down flat on the surface. The momentary resistance of the impact will give you enough support to push yourself back up.

Notice that it is the back, or non-power face, of the blade that is doing the work. To get it into position you may have to provide some wrist motion. When using a non-feathered paddle you will have to twist both wrists forward and straighten your arms to bring a blade into position for either a right- or left-side brace. When using a feathered paddle, the blade on the non-control-hand side is already in position for bracing. A brace on the control-hand side requires the wrist to be twisted forward and the arm straightened to position the blade. Here again is another example of the importance of keeping a set grip on the shaft.

Since you are pushing down for support the structure of your body requires that the paddle be just to your side, or slightly behind your hips, to be effective. The brace will work best when you are in the last half of a forward stroke or sitting with the paddle horizontal and waiting to respond to a possible capsize.

In either situation holding the paddle shaft as low and horizontal as possible is very important. When bracing, bring the paddle to hori-zontal and shift it laterally to the bracing side. Do not change your grip. You shift and, if need be, twist your wrists at the same time. Both arms will have elbows bent and raised, and the hand of the non-bracing arm held close to your stomach. Remain flexible at the waist, keeping the upper body vertical.

Using this extended lever, slap with the back of the blade. You only need to spank the water firmly, not beat it into submission. If it sounds like a a .357 Magnum has gone off, you've overdone it. Keep the other blade low, so the shaft stays level and the bracing blade hits as flat, and with as much surface area, as possible. Once it hits, push down to bring yourself and the boat back up.

Since the slap only gives momentary support you must regain your balance and recover the blade almost immediately. If you're fast, you can just pull the blade back to its starting position. But if you wait an instant too long, it begins to sink, losing its ability to bear your weight as it goes down. If you tried to pull the blade up while it was submerged, you would encounter the same resistance that braced you, resulting in a capsize by pulling yourself over. The only way to extract the blade is to rotate it to vertical by twisting your wrist back, then slicing the blade up and out as you push forward. The action is to roll the blade up, forward, and out. Recovery should be smooth, fast, and precise, without letting the blade sink too deeply.

For the slap brace to be effective it must become a reflex. Practice every chance you get: on both sides, eyes closed, or with the help of others standing next to the kayak trying to throw you off balance.

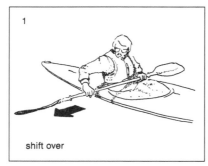

1

shift over

2

slap!

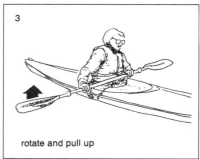

3

rotate and pull up

Low Brace

There's nothing inferior about this brace. The "low" in low brace refers only to the position of the hands, not its effectiveness. The term is also a designation for a family of strokes with similar traits. All low braces require you to push palms-down on the shaft, as if doing a push up, to get support. They also use the back, or non-power face, of the blade, and are held out to the side or rear quadrant. Besides the standard low brace there are two others: the slap, for quick recovery; and the sweeping, for longer support.

The low brace is directly related to the slap brace in that hand and arm positions are all basically the same. The only difference is that the low brace requires the boat to be moving so you can use the lift from a skimming blade for support. When thrown off balance while paddling forward, a low brace will give you plenty of assistance and time to recover. The paddle is held to the side with the bracing blade's leading edge tilted up. The blade's climbing angle produces lift that you can then lean on.

Blade angle is very important. Too steep an angle produces a lot of drag, which will slow the boat and not provide enough support. A very shallow angle gives lots of support with very little drag, but its leading edge can be easily tripped and suddenly changed to a diving angle. If this happens, immediately release your grip and let the blade go its own way, otherwise it will take you with it. In the beginning it is better to err on the side of caution. So use a good, steep climbing angle and work down from there.

To brace, hold the paddle shaft low and horizontal, extend it over the bracing side, and bring it down. When you feel the first signs of lift put your weight over the blade and push yourself up. The action is down and forward. To increase leverage you can pull up with the non-bracing arm while you push down with the bracing one. The result of all this is a very stable position as long as the boat keeps moving and the blade stays on the surface.

Eventually the kayak will slow to a point where the lift will no longer be adequate. Before this occurs, you should be up and retrieving the blade with an upward twisting of the wrist and a raising of the arms. As seen from the side, the blade skims forward, up, and out. If you don't make it up in time, the low brace can be linked into a sculling brace for continuous support as the boat stops.

Another linking possibility is with the stern rudder. By bringing the paddle a little more forward than is usual for a stern rudder and using the back of the blade with a climbing angle, you can perform what is known as a low brace turn. This imparts a wide arcing curve and gives enough support in the rear quadrant for you to lean the boat over to tighten the turn.

The skimming action of a low brace can also be used while you are being pushed sideways by a broadside wave or surf. To stabilize yourself, extend your paddle so it skims on top and a little behind the wave as you are driven sideways. It's a good way to keep from rolling over.

Sweeping Low Brace

There are times when you'll have to add some sweeping motion to a low brace to make up for its one major drawback: It is absolutely useless if the boat isn't moving through the water. Unlike the low brace which needs forward movement in order to function, the more dynamic sweeping low brace makes its own. Whenever you feel like you're losing it, with the kayak dead in the water or barely gliding to a stop, go to a sweep. Or use it to lean on when you need to take time out for a look around or to catch your breath.

Another good reason to add in some sweep is to increase the power of the brace. Like the reverse sweep stroke, the sweeping low brace uses the unwinding of the larger muscles of the torso. Anatomically this motion is very forceful and easy to execute. It's a power that comes from the upper body being directly centered over the paddle so you can really put your weight into it. This in turn enhances the stability of the stroke and your ability to recover. The stroke also swings the blade over a broad area, giving you a wide range of support. As you can see, the sweeping low brace is a very potent recovery tool and belongs in the front line of your defenses.

The sweep starts with the paddle shaft held low and close to horizontal. The bracing arm is practically straight with some bend to act as a shock absorber; the hand of the other arm is in close to the stomach. With the paddle extended like this the hand of the non-bracing arm acts like a pivot, with almost all power coming from the twisting of the body and some from the pushing of the bracing arm. Do not try to pull back with the inside hand as on a reverse sweep. Bring the back of the blade down as far to the rear as you can and swing it forward in a low, broad arc. Hold the shaft loosely and start the push with the heel of the palm. At the completion of the stroke, when the paddle is perpendicular to the boat or about even with your hips, withdraw the blade sharply with a firm push down and forward. If you are not already there, this last shove should bring you all the way back up.

As in other braces, blade angle will affect performance. The steeper the angle, the closer the stroke comes to being a reverse sweep and providing more turning force than lift. A flatter angle will give you more lift than directional control. There are nuances here that, for the sake of maximizing efficiency, should not be ignored.

Low braces, and in particular the sweeping low brace, are the most dependable and easiest to use of all the support or recovery strokes. They link in with almost every other stroke and make a good, general safety net that even experts fall back on when they find themselves over their heads.

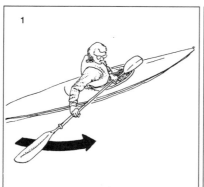

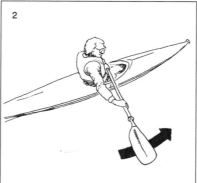

High Brace

Our bodies require a different type of stroke for bracing in the forward quadrant. From your hips forward, it is both awkward and ineffectual to try to push yourself up by the back of a blade. Your only option is to brace with the blade's power face. Recovery is made by pulling down on the shaft and hanging from it, as if doing a chin-up, with your palms facing up and elbows pointing down. While the low brace lets you get right over the paddle and push down with all your weight, the high brace offers less leverage but greater potential for recovery at extreme angles.

There is a danger, and a bit of an inconsistency, in thinking that a high brace should be held high. Actually, high braces should be performed quite low to the kayak. To do otherwise risks shoulder strain or even dislocation. So keep your high braces low, the paddle shaft as level as possible, elbows close to the body, and hands never going above the head.

For bracing on either side with a non-feathered paddle, or the control-hand side of a feathered paddle, blade angles are changed by twisting the wrist(s) back and, if needed, bringing the forearm(s) up. When bracing on the non-control-hand side of a feathered paddle you will have to rotate the blade through 180 degrees. This requires the moderate contortion of bringing your elbow forward, forearm up, hand to your shoulder, and twisting the wrist all the way back. It is a weak position but, if held near the body, will be safe.

The high brace is used with two kinds of blade motions, either a downward pull or a skimming sweep.

The downward pull is used when thrown off balance while paddling forward with the paddle anywhere forward of your hips. To catch yourself, reach out about three feet and slap the surface with the flat of the power face. Pull the blade down and towards you with the bracing arm, while using the other arm as a pivot held close to your body. As the blade goes deeper and the shaft angle steepens, there will be a corresponding reduction in support. If you're fast, or recover balance quickly, you will be able to pull the paddle in towards you and back to its starting position. If not, which is more likely, you will have to retrieve the blade by rotating it 90 degrees aft, slicing it up, and out.

Another downward pulling motion is used when thrown off balance by a broadside wave or surf that is too high for a low brace. Extend your paddle into the upper portion of the wave with a high brace, and as you are driven sideways, support comes from hanging on the shaft and pulling it downward.

A skimming sweep motion is used for the sweeping high brace, which can also be incorporated into the forward paddling stroke. It is a simple matter to convert the forward stroke into a brace by angling the blade back from vertical. Since there is no need to lift the blade, reaction time and your chance for recovery are excellent. With the proper climbing angle you'll get plenty of support over a broad arc, giving a usable range from all the way forward to just ahead of your hips. To the rear of this the brace weakens considerably until, just behind your hips, it is no longer viable. End the sweep by pulling your upper arm down and the lower arm back. This will slice the blade up and out aft. Or, you can link in with almost all of the propulsion, maneuvering, and even some of the low brace strokes.

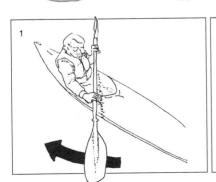  

Sculling Brace

Think of the sculling brace as a sweeping brace that just keeps on going. By moving the blade forward and back with its climbing angle switching each time it changes direction, you turn the paddle shaft into an unfaltering handle of support. With this you can maintain a firm stance or pull yourself up from some very extreme angles regardless of what is going on around you. Where slapping gave you a brief moment and sweeping a few seconds, sculling can provide support for as long as you keep the paddle in motion.

Not all unbalancing forces are short jabs; some, like the winds preceding a squall or waves caused by a tidal rip, can feel like a hand pressing down on you. To get through these you will have to take a prolonged defensive posture by leaning into them and sculling on the windward side. During a rescue or any other circumstance demanding stability for protracted periods, the sculling brace is again the one to opt for. There will also be times when you are knocked so far over as to make slapping or sweeping impossible. In these situations your only way out may be to scull yourself back up with this versatile and powerful brace.

A sculling brace need not always be a high brace. It can also be done by holding the paddle as if for a low brace. While this is a strong stroke, it cannot be used once the kayak has passed a rather shallow, heeling angle. It is therefore recommended that, for ultimate security at all angles, you learn and rely primarily on the high sculling brace.

The sculling motion must be thought of as constant, with every movement contributing to promoting lift, even during the switching of directions. The paddle is held out perpendicular to the boat and as close to horizontal as you can, providing the largest possible surface for lift. All power and sweeping motion comes from the hand and forearm on the bracing side, with the other hand held close to the body as a pivot for the shaft. Confine the stroke to a 45-degree arc (about a three foot sweep) directly to the side, going near neither bow nor stern.

The blade is kept on or near the surface, power face down, sweeping either forward or aft with the leading edge angled upwards.

Blade-angle switching is done as in feathering with a quick twist of the control-hand's wrist. The angle is always directed by the control hand (or hands, when using a non-feathered paddle). This is regardless of whether the control hand is in the upper or lower position. The cycle should be smooth and feel continuous, with no stopping where blade angles switch. Seen from the side the paddle inscribes an elongated figure eight. The blade climbs slightly upward during the stroke and then sharply downward as the angle is reversed. This keeps the pull steady and the motion uninterrupted.

Once perfected (this may take more strength and practice than other strokes) you will be able to hang from the paddle and lean way over; the further over you go, the more compressed the stroke. The figure-eight pattern will become flatter, and your strokes shorter and faster. It will take time to get to this point, but one of the nice things about practicing the sculling brace is that you have plenty of time to analyze what it is you are doing.

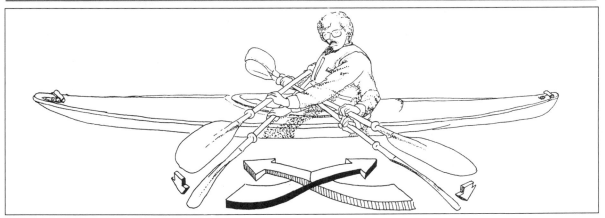

Sea Kayaking 102:

TOWARD THE HORIZON

If you've gotten this far, you're hooked! And it's a fortunate thing too, because what follows is the heart of sea kayaking: the good stuff. This is where the decisions are made, now that the preliminaries are out of the way. With what you'll learn in SK 102 you can start to better define what you are trying to get from the sport. You'll also be able to make informed choices about equipment and evaluate the opinions of "experts."

Or, you can, as many do, forget about what follows and get by with what you have learned so far.

That's fine if it gives you what you are looking for. But there are those who look toward the horizon. It can be any horizon, distant or personal. Since horizons are by nature unattainable, there are no set goals; only the pleasure of doing something well. That's what SK 102 is all about, and why its tone is a bit more personal than authoritative.

In SK 101 you learned the basics because you had to if you were going to use a kayak. But in SK 102 there is nothing that you *have* to do, it is all up to you. From here on, only you can set the benchmarks of your progress.

Although 102 is not structured as such, it can be thought of as an introduction to the principles of circles of defense. These circles are nothing more than intentionally redundant safety measures. As one fails, another surfaces. It is a timeless tradition of the sea not to put your faith in any one skill or object. It is the philosophy of the realist. Know your ship, the waters you sail on, yourself, and be prepared for anything.

Some equipment, while not necessary, can make paddling easier and safer. It is a good outer circle of defense. Get the best you can afford, get what you need, think of what might go wrong, and then get things to help with that.

There is something very satisfying about equipment. It is almost as if you were buying security. Most of it looks so dependable and reassuring, and used wisely it can be. But very often the passion for equipment is the hiding place of those hoping to purchase what can only be achieved. Choose products with discretion, use them wisely, but in the end don't put a whole lot of faith in them.

When the magic of purchased material fails, you have to fall back to the next circle of defense: Your skill as a paddler. This is the best place to center your energies and hopes. Soon you will begin to understand how much more seaworthy you and your kayak can be. It's about control. You'll no longer be reacting to what the boat does to you. From now on, it will be the boat reacting to what you do to it. This is true mastery of your vessel and it's a little scary because your limits become very obvious. A good seaman understands these limitations and works with them. A poor seaman is clouded in vanity and has an unrealistic vision of his capabilities. Stay objective, practice and paddle with others, and respect what you don't know.

The Eskimo Roll can be one of your last circles of defense. As a means of capsize recovery, it is a skill of last resort and an art unto itself. It is challenging to learn; many paddlers never do. While not absolutely necessary, it does bring a feeling of command which affects how you approach the sport.

Probably the most important circle of defense is your understanding of the waters you paddle on. In the pages that follow you'll explore your environment and learn the basics of good seamanship. What you'll find is a good start—the rest will take time and experience. It's an education that never ends and always fascinates. Bon voyage!

WHAT YOU WILL NEED

Advanced Gear

Clothing

The problem with dressing for kayaking is that you have to take into account three separate environments: the air, the water, and the inside of the kayak sealed by the spray skirt. Almost none have compatible comfort and protection requirements. While the air may be one temperature it is not uncommon for the water to vary by 40 degrees, usually lower, making your body from the waist down either nice and snug or hot and steamy.

If conditions are moderate and your bracing and rolling skills are in top form, you can eliminate at least one of these variables. If there is no need to dress for extended immersions, your only worries will be the outside air and the inside of the kayak, not the water: that is, not the water directly below you. You'll still be getting wet from spray and an occasional wave, but this can be taken care of by a lightweight paddling jacket. If the air is warm, you may not even want that, doing just fine in a bathing suit and tee shirt.

As the air cools or wind increases (wind chill), clothing for your upper body becomes more important. The best way to approach this problem is with a system of layering clothes. The layer closest to your skin needs to be breathable. A non-moisture-absorbing material that will allow perspiration to evaporate out of contact with your skin should be used as a base layer in cold weather. Cotton is one of the worst fabrics for this job. It readily absorbs moisture, is a poor insulator when wet, and dries slowly so you stay cold longer. This makes it a poor choice for cold weather, but for tropical paddling it is ideal, also offering good sun protection. The best base layer fabrics are open weaves of impermeable fibers like polypropylene or polyester. They dry quickly and do not absorb perspiration. A single layer of this may be all you'll need from the spray skirt down.

As it gets colder you will want to add intermediate layers. Take caution about overdoing it, for once you start paddling you will become your own heat source. What feels comfortable on the beach might be too much underway. If there is any question, don't wear the item but bring it along so you can stop and change into

it later. When camping or spending any time on land, extra cold-weather gear will keep you properly dressed when not active. That's the nice thing about layering: it's adjustable.

The purpose of this intermediate layer is to create a thermal barrier, an air trap for insulation. Bulky and loosely woven fleece-like fabrics like synthetic pile or wool work best.

The final outer layer should act as a vapor lock, keeping air in for improved insulation. It also has to keep you and your clothing dry. Moisture comes from within in the form of perspiration, so there has to be good ventilation. Moisture comes from without in the form of spray and waves, so there has to be good waterproofing and tight seals. These conflicting needs are hard to satisfy.

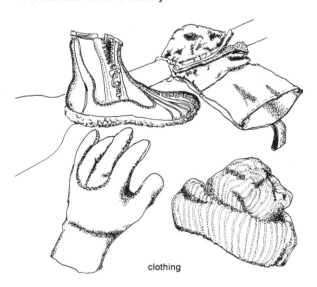

clothing

You'll have to take care of your extremities, too. Head, hands, and feet all require protection at one time or an other.

Head gear in warm weather can be anything that will keep the sun off, won't blow away, and can be soaked in water to be worn wet for keeping cool. In colder weather more than half of your body heat is lost through the head. So by taking your hat on and off you have a manually adjustable thermostat. Probably the best hat is a wool watch cap. Hoods on paddling jackets or wind breakers are good for wind and rain protection and work well if they do not restrict head motion. As an alternative to a hood some folks use the traditional Sou'wester rain hat. They are less restrictive of motion, but tend to make the wearer look like a character on the box of frozen fish sticks.

Hands do best when they are kept dry and, in extreme conditions, warm. Your first defense is good and well-placed drip rings on the paddle shaft. In rain or heavy weather you might want to try gloves. No one type seems to be a panacea. Everybody makes do with something of their own devising. Driving, dish-washing, sailing, or work gloves all have been used. The challenge is to stay warm and dry without sacrificing grip. In really cold weather hands can be sealed up in gadgets called Pogies. These are gauntleted mittens which fit around the shaft. You slip your hands in and grip the shaft directly.

Even though they are safely tucked away down in the sealed cockpit, feet also need some protection. Their biggest hardship is in getting the kayak to and from the water. Again the field is wide open. Paddlers have used neoprene wet suit booties, sandals, socks, old sneakers (keep laces short so they don't get caught), boots, or the new, specially-made, water sport shoes for wind surfing. One is as good, or bad, as the next depending on your usage. What gets you across a beach of jagged rocks and cold water, may become an insufferable mold factory when sealed in the kayak. Another problem is abrasion on your heels from the inside of the hull. Very few pieces of foot gear are protected in this area, so you might have to pad the hull where your heels touch. This gives the added benefit of improved boat control through another solid contact point and, if the weather is warm, the ability to get by barefooted.

Paddling Jacket

These have been designed to act as the final outer skin in your layering system. They are reminiscent of the original Eskimo anorak which covered the paddler from his hooded head down to where it bellied out to be very

securely fastened around the cockpit coaming. It was as watertight as possible, and pretty much kept you trapped in the kayak no matter what.

Today's paddling jacket is a little more forgiving and versatile than the old anorak. It is

paddling jacket

also not intended to be absolutely watertight, being worn over the spray skirt and sealed by only a cord or elastic around the waist. If you capsize, some water will find its way in as you roll back up. This is acceptable as its purpose is only to shed waves and spray, provide a dead air space for insulation, and also (unlike the anorak) provide some ventilation. Excess heat and body moisture were no problems to the Eskimos, but for us paddling in more hospitable waters it can be a nuisance. So a good paddling jacket should have ways to let you vent off this built-up steam.

The material should be lightweight, waterproof nylon or something similar. Be suspicious of miracle breathable/waterproof fabrics. Most ocean sailors and kayakers have found that "breathing" stops early on when the fabric gets choked with salt.

Fit should be loose around the shoulders and upper arms to allow unrestricted motion and roomy around the body to leave room for undergarments. You'll want wrist openings to be as waterproof as possible to keep annoying paddle drips from rolling down your arms. Neoprene is the most commonly used material with adjustable velcro tabs to keep the seal tight. Elastic knitted materials won't work at all, absorbing water and stretching out of shape. Neck closures are a bit tricky in that a really good seal can almost strangle you. Absolute watertight integrity is not important here because we want to be able to release built-up body heat and moisture. Look for a high, mandarin collar design, maybe with a hood. Since the garment is not going to be absolutely waterproof it is safest if the waist is not sealed. A completely closed jacket could hold enough water to drag you down. Drawstrings and toggles or elastics are adequate.

Nice extras are a velcro-sealable pouch in front, pocket on the sleeve, opening and closing vents, and a detachable or stowaway hood.

Wet suit

When sea conditions deteriorate, water temperatures go below 60 degrees F, or there is any chance of having to spend a prolonged time in the water (no matter what the temperature), your choice of what to wear becomes a lot more serious than just comfort. Water draws heat away from the body at a rate 25 percent faster than air. Even in the tropics a long time spent in the water can be debilitating.

One of the most popular ways of protecting yourself from loss of body heat is with some form of wet suit. The Neoprene they are made from contains tiny air bubbles, making it both a good insulator and a source of flotation. Additional insulation comes from a thin layer of water which is heated by your body. Even in air they are good insulators and can be used as part of a layering system. Their only drawback for this use is that they retain moisture and become uncomfortably clammy after awhile. This can be improved upon by using inner-layer clothing like polypropylene underwear or any synthetic, open knit, stretchy fabric underneath the neoprene.

Fit is obviously an important factor. It must be snug enough to hold as small an amount of water as possible, but not so tight that movement is difficult. Before buying, try sitting to make sure you can still breathe and aren't being confined in the seat or crotch. Suits come in thicknesses from 1/8 inch for warm water paddling, to 3/16 inch for general purpose use, to 1/4 inch for colder waters. The last choice is quite thick and may even hold back body rotation. Check first before buying. Your choices in wet suits are:

Full wet suit. Used mostly for diving, these are not suitable for sea kayaking because they make free arm and upper body motion too difficult. No wet suit used for paddling should have arms. These should be removed and the opening cut deep below the armpits to allow full arm rotation.

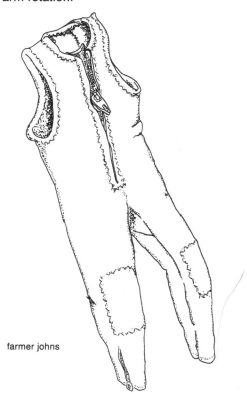

farmer johns

Farmer johns. These are like a full wet suit with its arms cut off at the shoulder, leaving a bib in front and a high back. This gives you good protection and freedom of movement. Because they cover so much of the body, 3/16-inch farmer johns and a paddling jacket might be sufficient for year-round kayaking in moderate climates.

Shorty. Same as above but with the legs cut off just above the knees. They keep the body's core protected and are good to extend the season on each side of summer.

Vest. Cover only the absolute minimum and are good for light summer duty, or under a dry suit. Some vests are fitted with nylon sleeves to make a practical variation on the paddling jacket theme.

Hood. Separate hoods, while uncomfortable and limiting of head motion, can help the head retain heat in severe weather. For some, the loss of good hearing is a detriment; small holes or cut-outs can be made to help.

Wet suits only work when you wear them. If the conditions are serious enough to warrant the use of one, put it on before going out. Trying to climb into the suit after a dunking is the height of folly. It's almost impossible to do, and the impact of the cold water will have already taken its toll.

Dry Suit

If you are trying to stay warm in cold water, it is better to be dry than wet. Ideally, a dry suit lets you dress in the right clothing for the day and then cover that with a watertight suit. Unlike neoprene, the dry suit has no insulating properties. It depends solely on the clothing it is protecting and the enclosed dead-air space to keep you warm. And they will keep you warm, much warmer than a wet suit. Dry suits are a serious step toward cold-water protection. The fact that you are even considering a dry suit indicates that you plan to encounter some very serious sea conditions and water whose temperature may be substantially below 50 degrees F. Putting on a dry suit usually means you are committing yourself to a potentially dangerous situation. Give it some thought before proceeding.

Also, give some thought to not wearing a dry suit. With moderate water temperatures and minimal risks of immersion, a too-efficient dry suit can cook you like a pork chop in a Shake n' Bake bag. Overdressing, especially in a dark colored suit on a sunny day, can result in heat exhaustion.

There is no doubt that keeping water away is your best cold-weather defense. But all defenses have their price and, as a starter, dry suits are more expensive than wet suits. For this money you do get a lot more cold water

dry suit

protection and comfort. If the right clothes are used, and it is best to dress a little light because you will be generating your own heat, a dry suit can provide the perfect environment.

Dry is also a very relative term concerning these suits. With a persistent dampness coming from body heat and moisture that has no where to go, it is very difficult to both vent a suit and keep it perfectly watertight. In fact, it is hard to keep a suit perfectly watertight at all. The fabric is usually no problem; it's the seals.

Seals at the wrists, ankles, and neck have to do a tough job. They are intended to stop the circulation of air and water without cutting off the circulation of blood. Entry zippers on one-piece suits also bring their share of potential problems and leaks. Rear-entry suits seem to leak less than the front-entry type, but require help putting on. Surprisingly, some of the most waterproof suits are the two piece variety because the sealing between the jacket and pants can be done so well. Some of these suits also give you the important option of using the jacket on its own.

A dry suit's fit should be roomy enough to cover a full range of clothing, but not so bulky as to get in the way when paddling. Too much air held in the suit can be awkward or even dangerous when swimming. Consider what might happen with a lot of air trapped in the legs. This is why dry suits have to be "burped" to expel all excess air.

Luckily, because of the growing popularity of board sailing and sea kayaking, there are plenty of dry suits available. But avoid the heavier suits for diving. They are too restrictive and unnecessarily expensive. Whichever type you choose, think long and hard before buying. You may not even really need one.

Visual Distress Signals

Nobody likes to talk about dire emergencies in sea kayaking; although exceedingly rare, they do happen. There may come a time in your paddling career when you are overwhelmed by circumstances. It can happen to anyone through a lapse of judgment or a surprise occurrence. While not pleasant to think about, it is best to acknowledge the possibility and prepare for it. By doing this you will keep yourself realistically outfitted and in compliance with the law.

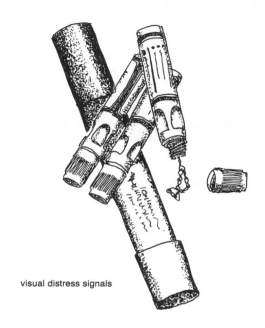

visual distress signals

For some unexplained reason, the U.S. Coast Guard requires kayaks to carry visual distress signals only at night, while all other vessels must be equipped with them at all times. Who knows what they had in mind and why only at night, but legally we have to carry some sort of signaling device between sunset and dawn. This includes all inland waters and the Great Lakes, too.

You are given three options: an electric distress light, which is a high-intensity flashlight that automatically sends the SOS code four to six times per minute; a strobe light; or pyrotechnics. The first two options are the least practical for kayaking. They do not command immediate attention, have limited range low in the water, and are adversely affected by conditions of poor visibility. The last option, commonly called flares, are the best. They have none of the disadvantages of the first two and an advantage that they are also useful during the day. To meet regulations there must be at least three hand-held or aerial flares aboard labeled as being Coast Guard approved, with an expiration date that does not exceed 42 months from the date of manufacture (not purchase), and stowed to be "readily available."

WHAT YOU WILL NEED

When a situation occurs that warrants the use of flares keep in mind the two stages of a rescue: to alarm and to direct. Alarming devices have to get people to stop, turn around, and look, which can be a surprisingly difficult job even in urban areas. To do this, use aerial flares which overcome your limited line of sight and make a loud noise at the same time. Once you've gotten their attention, you have to keep rescuers aware of your position so they can be directed to you. To do this, use hand-held flares or smoke generators.

Aerial flares are mostly for alarming. The ideal is to get something bright as high up as possible for as long as possible and to make some noise while doing it. There are a wide variety available that are made mostly for yachting, such as self-contained launcher/flares. More versatile, but clumsier to deal with and needing two hands to use, are the 25-mm flare pistols which can send up all sorts of rocketry. There are meteors which are brief flaming balls that go high up and then directly down, or parachutes which make a loud bang at altitude and then descend slowly. If you are going to bother carrying this sort of equipment, do not go half way with only a 12-gauge gun, for the devices it shoots are not worth the trouble.

A popular alternative to guns are the small pencil meteor flares. They are sold in packages of three (so they complete the minimum Coast Guard requirements) that can fit in your pocket, are relatively inexpensive, and each has its own built-in launcher. They are a compromise of duration and brightness for convenience. To compensate, carry a lot of them. When shooting any aerial flare, hold the launcher above your head and point it into the wind at a 60 degree angle to the horizon.

Directing, or the ability to guide rescuers and pinpoint your position, is best done with either hand-held flares or smoke-generating devices. Unlike aerial flares, the hand-held type last for longer periods and are less affected by winds. But, since they are low to the water, they offer a limited range of signal visibility. These flares work equally well in day or night conditions, while smoke-generating devices are only for daylight use. The U.S. Coast Guard approves only those generators, hand-held or

floating canisters, that put out smoke, usually orange, for at least 50 seconds. In bright sunlight on windless days smoke can be the best overall device for alarming and directing. Given a chance, the smoke cloud will rise to impressive heights and linger for some time over you. In less favorable conditions the smoke cloud may be held close to the surface or rapidly dispersed by strong winds. The smoke may also be impossible to see when looking into the sun or wind.

A good minimal distress package would consist of two parachute flares to alarm, three to six pencil meteor flares to alarm at close distances and to direct, one hand-held flare for day or night directing, and a smoke generator for day directing.

All flares and signaling devices, even if they are designated "marine," are susceptible to the ravages of moisture and salt. They have to be carefully stowed away and protected to remain viable. But they also have to be available when needed, the instant they are needed, without having to remove the spray skirt, digging into sacks, or anything else. The best arrangement is to carry some alarming signals on your person at all times. Use PFD or jacket pockets, or clip a small one to the PFD. Keep the rest of the alarming signals on deck in a watertight container like a ziplock bag and the directing signals inside the boat if there is no room on deck.

Flares can cause as much trouble as they try to resolve. Many hand-held flares drip molten slag as they burn, which can melt your skin or the kayak's. Hold the flares high on the downwind side and at an angle over the water. Even worse are the flares that do nothing. A high percentage of pyrotechnics are duds and you never know which ones they are until you try to light them (a good reason to carry more than you think you'll need). If a flare should fail to go off immediately, hold on to it for a few extra seconds. If it still does not ignite, throw it in the water and forget about it. Keep flares locked away from kids. Kids love them and are fully capable of sending up a warning rocket in your living room (which will get more results and attract more attention than any flare you'll ever launch on the water).

Light

If you're traveling at night, it makes sense to carry a flashlight. It is also the law. The Coast Guard in their eternal benevolence has seen fit to exempt kayaks from having to install electric red and green navigation lights. Your only obligation as a paddler is to have at hand "... a white light which shall be exhibited in sufficient time to prevent collision." Although not specified, the range of this light should be two miles. Keep the light secured in some way on deck so it is ready at a moment's notice. Obviously waterproofing (not just water-resistance) and high intensity are desirable features.

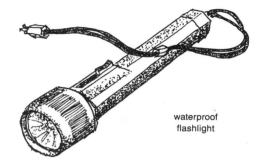

waterproof
flashlight

EXPLORING YOUR LIMITS

Knee Lift

Dynamic stability (see page 49) uses body motion to keep the kayak upright. What we'll explore here draws on the same principles. But instead of you reacting to what the boat does, it will now be the boat that does the reacting. This is about controlling the side to side tilt of the kayak with your knees.

There are two ways to tilt a kayak. The first is called "leaning," which is done by holding your upper and lower body as one unit and leaning over. The result is that the boat, as well as your body, goes over on an angle. This type of tilting puts your center of gravity off to one side and is inherently unstable unless used to compensate for forces in a fast turn (like a motorcycle rider going around a corner), which rarely occur in sea kayaking. A more stable and controlled way to tilt a kayak is by "edging." This is done by staying flexible at your waist to separate the upper from the lower body. The tilting force comes from your lower body pushing up through the knees while the upper body stays perpendicular to the water. The knee lifts up one side of the boat and the boat tilts while your center of gravity stays over it. You can get the kayak over to some very extreme angles this way without losing balance or control.

What good is all this knee lifting? It can be used to raise a side of the kayak to slide over the water when going sideways with a draw or sculling stroke. It can tilt the boat over to get its ends out of the water, reducing the boat's waterline length and making stationary or moving turns easier. It can be used to turn the kayak while underway and is useful in waves or surf. When incorporated into any of the bracing strokes a knee lift can provide that extra punch to bring you back up or can be used on its own for less drastic recoveries.

To knee lift a boat onto its side, bring the knee up on the side you want to raise. This is a lifting motion that starts by flexing the foot and raising the hip on the side to be raised, while depressing the hip and buttock on the other side. You are literally lifting one side of the boat so it is hanging from your knee while you are balancing on your lower buttock. As a test, try alternately lifting one knee and then the other to rock the kayak. The sensation is that your hips are moving up and down, but actually it is your knees that are controlling the motion.

As with earlier examples of dynamic stability, a flexible connection between upper and lower bodies is the key. To keep balanced, your upper body has to stay upright and over the boat's center of buoyancy. Lean the boat, not your body. Since knee lifting employs muscles not commonly used, exercises that strengthen and stretch your torso can help. For example do a knee lift on one side and hold the boat on edge for as long as you can. Repeat on the other side.

How you fit within the kayak is critical to the success of a knee lift. Your lower body, from the hips down, should be connected to the boat. When it moves, the boat must move. Movement comes primarily from your groin, back, and abdominal muscles, and is directed to the boat through your knees, and to a lesser extent your thighs if there is a good thigh-bracing system. When lifting, your knee will be supporting most of the boat's weight. There will be times when even greater forces must be absorbed from the momentum of a knee being driven up hard to prevent a capsize. So, the boat's knee braces must be well padded and strong.

push up with knee,
down with hip

Carved Turns

One of the most irritating experiences is trying to hold a course in a side wind when your boat wants to weathercock into it. You have to constantly work against the kayak's tendency to turn into the wind, which forces you to paddle harder or more frequently on one side, which in turn slows you down, ruins your paddling rhythm, and leaves you with sore muscles. In most cases a carved turn can eliminate, or at least reduce, this tiresome problem.

The carved turn works by leaning the kayak enough to change its underwater shape to affect how it steers. If the boat is leaned to the left, the pressures on the now asymmetrical shape of its waterline causes it to veer to the right. Try this on your own boat. Get going at a good clip and stop paddling when you feel you are going straight. If the boat is level, it should continue on course. Do this again, but when you stop paddling, knee lift the boat so it leans to one side. More than likely the boat will slowly turn away from the side the boat was tilted towards.

Most kayaks will respond in varying degrees. Some may have to be tilted way over before turning. Others are so seriously out of fore-and-aft trim, or of such an extreme design, that they will yaw off in an ever-tightening circle. Thankfully, these are rare cases.

In use, you would be paddling along and realize that you are putting more of an effort than you'd like into fighting the boat. To compensate tilt up the downwind side with a knee lift and continue paddling forward. If the wind is not too strong, your carved turn might be enough to counteract the boat's weathercocking. If it is not, you will have to paddle with a slight sweep stroke on the upwind side. This will be easy to do now that the side you are sweeping on has been lowered and you are still in an upright and efficient paddling position. Or, you can lean the boat over only when you make a stroke: upwind stroke, upwind lean; downwind stroke, no lean. If you want to increase your leaning, add a bracing angle to the blade for extra support as you sweep. The same techniques can be used for preventing broaches while paddling downwind or to make small course corrections in calm water.

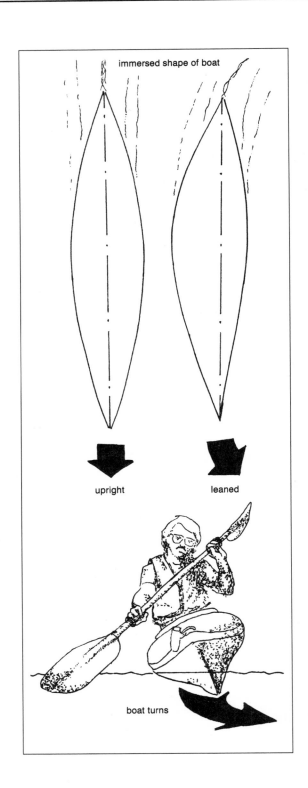

immersed shape of boat

upright   leaned

boat turns

Hip Flick

There is a fine line between a knee lift and a hip flick, so fine that many kayakers do not even bother making the distinction. Terminology is, after all, relatively unimportant. What is important is visualizing that your knees do the lifting for the powerful muscles around your waist. If your upper body can be supported by something, such as a solid bracing stroke, then the lower body and the boat it is attached to can be moved by the muscles in your torso. When these muscles are flexed (flicked) their momentum, coupled with the driving up of the knees, can force a boat over as well as bring it back up. Although it is the abdominal muscles doing the work, it feels like it's coming from your hips. Which is why it's called a hip flick.

To learn the hip flick, you'll need a controlled environment and a friend standing by just in case. Find a pool, low dock, ladder on a dock, or get your friend to stand in chest-deep water holding a paddle horizontal on the surface. What you're looking for is something solid to hold on to. Once you've learned the hip flick you'll substitute a dependable bracing stroke for this solid training support.

Grab the support with both hands, palms facing down. Lean your body so your head, shoulders, and torso are in the water. Pull the kayak over onto its edge and hold it there just before the point of capsize. To bring the boat back up, hold your upper body in place and give a twisting flick at your waist, forcing the knee up against the low side of the boat. By connecting this flick to your lower body, and then through your knees to the kayak, you should impart enough of a sudden push to rotate the boat upright. It will feel as if the boat has been rolled back under you, and it has.

In the beginning there are two instincts which you must fight. The first is not to use the strength of your arms to pull yourself up, but the twisting of your torso muscles to rotate the boat. Ignore your arms as much as possible. They are there only to provide a point of balance. Your upper body should be completely isolated from the process, with all lifting and righting moments coming from the hip flick. You'll find that once you get the hang of it, you'll only need to hold the support with your finger tips, feeling no strain at all on your arms.

The second instinct to fight is bringing your head up first. Your head should be the last thing to leave the water as you roll up. Intuitively we want to get our heads up to breathe. But by doing so you work against righting the kayak. While in the water the head and torso are buoyed up, so they weigh less. Also, if the head and torso come up too soon, they raise your center of gravity, making it harder for the boat to right. The idea is to flick the boat up with enough follow-through that it carries your body and head along with it. The rising order should be the boat followed by your waist, torso, shoulders, and, lastly, your head.

Once you have the feel from a near capsize position, try a hip flick with the boat fully inverted. Holding on as before, capsize towards the support side. Once capsized you will experience tremendous stretching at your waist as you simultaneously hold your body near the surface and try to keep seated in the overturned kayak. Think of yourself as a taut spring being stretched to its limits. When ready, give your waist a sudden and sustained twist so this powerful spring can return to its coiled position, pushing your knee and the boat upwards.

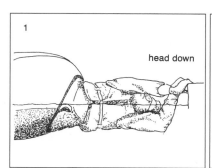

1

head down

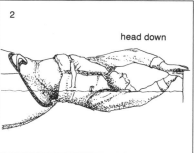

2

head down

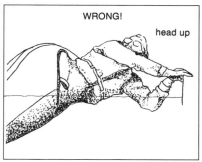

WRONG!

head up

Extended Bracing

The bracing stroke is a reaction to "oops!," the feeling that you are going over. An extended bracing stroke is the reaction to "oh my God!," the feeling that you are really going over and might not be coming back. Exploring your limits means you're also going to have to extend your bracing. As you push your abilities further you'll find newer and more interesting ways of getting into trouble. Extended bracing will help you get out of them.

Extended bracing is a response to a critical situation. It's a holding action, giving a solid support from which to hip flick back up. It can also help maintain a defensive posture when overwhelmed and provide stability while performing unwieldy tasks or rescuing others. Obviously, it's good to learn how to extend oneself.

There are three ways of extending a brace. You can extend the paddle, your body, or combine the two.

Extending the paddle means altering your grip on the shaft. For general paddling it is not a good policy to move your hands about. But things are not always that simple, and there will be times when you will want, or need, to maximize the paddle's leverage. Do this by shifting your hands upward along the shaft. Bring the upper hand to the throat of the upper blade and the lower hand to the middle of the shaft. To help your orientation use the crook of the little finger of the upper hand to feel the edge of the blade. Maintain the same hand spacing as usual, and try to keep the shaft close in for the most effective use of your strength. An interesting variation of the extended paddle brace is to reverse it and substitute the crook of your shoulder for the center grip. This lets you scull with one hand while you go about your chores with the other.

Extending your body requires immersing as much of your upper body and head as possible. This may sound contradictory since the idea of bracing is to stay out of the water. But if you've gone too far over, you may have no choice. Or you may do it intentionally. For Greenland Eskimos in their ultra-narrow kayaks this was standard procedure. By sculling and utilizing the body's natural buoyancy they could hold in a very stable attitude for quite some time.

Trying to brace at extreme angles with your upper body hanging out over the paddle requires a lot of energy. You're asking the stroke to support almost your full weight. By lowering your head and upper body into the water you reduce their weight through buoyancy and at the same time lower your center of gravity. This makes it easier to keep the kayak from going all the way over and gives you the time and security to bring yourself back up.

To get in position while bracing, twist at the waist so your back is to the water and you are leaning toward the rear of the boat. Face upward, keeping the back of your head in the water. It's like doing a back float while in the kayak. Once you've learned to relax in this nearly-capsized position you'll find that you can maintain it for quite some time. During all this the kayak will have a tendency to move about. Use your lower body and knees to keep it under control. When ready to come up give a powerful hip flick and pull down on the paddle. Remember that the boat comes up first, followed by your torso, and, lastly, by your head.

You have to dedicate yourself fully to an extended brace in order for it to succeed. When you feel yourself going over don't give up. Try to brace, and brace hard. Be willing to fight and commit yourself to the brace. Extend the paddle, lower your head and body, and scull or pull up for all you're worth. For your first attempts you might want to practice in shallow water where you can push off the bottom if you can't hold the brace. It takes effort, finesse, timing, and balance to make an extended brace work, but in the end it will do the job.

ESKIMO ROLL

Principles

There's nothing wrong with capsizing. It shows that you're exploring your limits, and that's good. The only problem is that each time you capsize you've got to get out, get in, and start over again. Not exactly energy efficient, or fun. Plus the thought of going through all that might make you afraid to take chances or experiment—and that's *not* good.

A way of recovering from a capsize without leaving the boat is the Eskimo roll. The principle behind the roll is simple. Once over, you sweep the paddle out as a bracing stroke from which you can pull and hip flick your way back up. Simple. At least it should be.

For some, rolling is one of the most difficult skills to master. It is disorienting to hang upside down, and there are a lot of motions that have to interact perfectly for it to work. Many kayakers never do learn to roll and that's OK; you may not even have to learn how. If you paddle a folding or very wide kayak that is ultra stable, or paddle only in settled surroundings, rolling may never be necessary.

There seems to be some mystical image that goes with the Eskimo roll. Yet, contrary to popular belief, not all the aboriginal kayaking traditions included this ability. The Aleuts never used the roll, practicing a reentry method instead, and they got on fine for a few thousand years. It is not the end-all of rescue techniques. As long as you have one or two other ways of recovering, you'll get by.

But without it you will subconsciously develop a style that is interested more in staying upright than in efficiency. This makes you paddle defensively and plateau out way below your natural level of ability. When you can roll, you become more self-sufficient and less anxious when things start to go wrong. Compared with other rescue methods rolling is quick, works in rough water, reduces exposure, and requires a minimal outlay of energy. If you can, learn how to roll.

The Eskimo roll is not a superhuman feat, nor is it an advanced maneuver only for experts. It demands no more strength and skill than a strong brace. In essence, a roll is only a sweeping brace done upside down.

Once inverted, the paddler sets up with his body leaning forward and upward against the deck, his paddle on the surface ready to make a broad, sweeping brace stroke. As the sweep starts to bring up the boat, the paddler hip flicks to bring it the rest of the way. When the kayak is almost upright the body and head are brought up with a forceful brace or draw at the end of the sweep.

The first recorded roll by a non-Eskimo was in 1927 by the Austrian Hans Pawlata, who picked up the idea from the writings of Arctic explorers. Not only was he the first but he was also one of the few who have ever learned to roll from a book. Teaching yourself to roll is neither easy nor safe. With the information in this section, and some real dedication, you could learn to roll without anyone's help. But it's unlikely.

If you can, get a knowledgeable instructor or someone to use as a role (roll) model who will coach you. At the very least have a concerned friend standing by.

There are many types of rolls. The one described here is a modified screw roll, so called because paddlers look like they are twisting through the water like a screw. It is one of the simplest and most reliable. There is no universal "best" roll, but it's close to it.

The roll can be explained by breaking it into its component parts. Learn them one at a time, while keeping in mind the place each has in the total process. When you can perform all the components, combine them into a full roll.

Before starting, you'll need to have the hip flick and extended high brace down pat. These two points are the foundation of all rolling. You'll also find a nose clip or face mask invaluable. Practice in warm water with all your gear (PFD, etc.) on, and rest frequently to keep from getting dizzy. Almost anyone who puts his or her mind to it can roll. Even you.

Practice: Set Up

The unnerving thing about a capsize is how suddenly it occurs. One moment you're breathing air, the next you're wishing you were one step back on the evolutionary ladder and had gills. I don't know if it's more of a shock when it's rough and you're expecting it, or when it's calm and it's the furthest thing from your mind. Either way, the first steps in having a foolproof roll start with being able to set up, whether you're in a maelstrom or on a pond.

If you have practiced regularly and with dedication the set-up position could become instinctual. But since very few of us are that obsessively devoted to rolling, it should at least become mechanical. Get your set up to where it can be done by the numbers and you'll be alright. The best way is to develop a pattern and do it step-by-step each time, every time.

Before starting you will have to choose which side to set up on. Most paddlers find that their "good" side is the one opposite from their control hand. If your feathering is controlled by the right hand, set up on the left side. If you are paddling non-feathered, decide which side your brace and hip flick is strongest on and set up on the opposite side. If your strongest high brace is on the left, set up on the right. Once you've got that settled, sit in the kayak and go through the set up step-by-step.

The first step is twisting at the waist to get the paddle over the side and parallel to the boat.

The second step is to slide your rear hand to the base of the rear blade and your forward hand to the center of the shaft. Hold the base of the rear blade with your palm on its power face. You can usually tell the power face by tactile clues such as its curve or center ridge. If not, provide a clue with tape.

The third step sets up the angle of the forward blade, so its outer edge is angled upward to provide lift as it sweeps around. Practicing rightside up, the outer edge will be angled downward. Your rear hand is the key to getting the correct blade angle. With feathered paddles the rear hand, with palm on the power face, is held with knuckles down and fingernails on the boat's side at the seam line (or gunwale). With non-feathered paddles use the same grip but keep your wrist cocked back so its underside touches the seam line. Check the forward blade to see that its power face is up (down while practicing) and that it is on about a 30-degree angle. Record this rear hand position in your mind.

The fourth step places the underside of the wrist of your forward hand on the seam line. This puts the shaft on a slight angle pointing up (or down, when practicing rightside up) and out, away from the hull.

The fifth step is to lean forward as far as possible. If you can, bring your nose to the deck. In this tucked-in position your head is protected and you are closer to the boat's axis of rotation, making it easier for you to right yourself.

That's it. Remember these five points, practice them with your eyes closed, going strictly by feel, and you'll automatically get yourself into the set-up position. To see if you've got it right, try setting up and capsizing. Have someone of reasonable strength stand next to you in waist-deep water. Get in the set-up position and capsize. As you go over keep your arms pressed tightly against the hull and exhale slowly through your nose; or wear a nose clip or face mask. When over, extend both hands as high as you can to get the paddle well clear of the water. To make sure that your forward blade is free, try to slap it on the surface. Have your helper check for blade angle and to see that the rear blade is held high enough to clear the boat's bottom during the sweep. When ready to come up, hit the boat three times. Your helper should reach over the bottom of the upturned kayak, grab its side, and pull you over. You can help by staying in a tucked position.

As a final test, capsize while in the normal paddling position and go to the set up after you've capsized. You'll find that the paddle winds up in the strangest places. Just stop, collect your thoughts for a second, and go through the steps one-by-one.

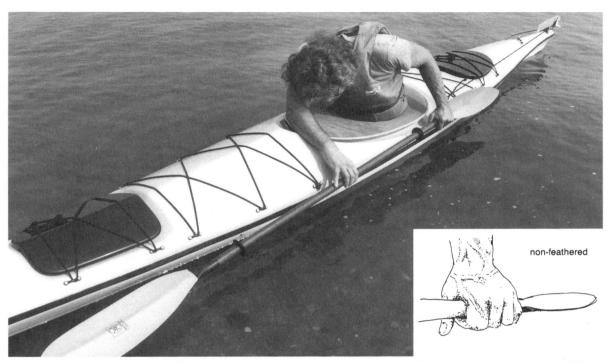

non-feathered

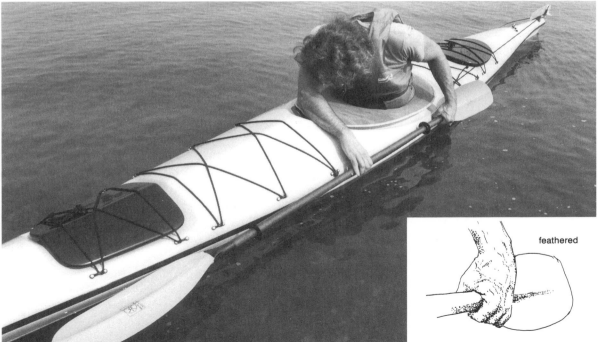

feathered

Practice: Sweep

The blade's sweep across the water provides a supporting brace that gets you and the kayak most of the way up, and the paddle into position for the hip flick. It is one of the trickiest maneuvers in kayaking, and definitely worthy of some extra help while practicing. The best place to get this help is from a solid-foam paddle float and an assistant.

When your float and assistant are all set, capsize with your helper standing off to the side you will sweep out on. When completely inverted go through the steps of setting up, making sure to push both hands well above the water. Keep the rear arm bent and held high enough so the rear blade will clear the boat's bottom; check to see that the forward blade is in place by slapping it on the surface. To produce lift, the leading edge of the forward blade must be raised. Check that your rear wrist is in the proper position and cock your forward wrist to impart the proper angle.

Start the sweep with conviction and speed. The forward arm is almost straight and is swung around like a gate. The other arm should push up and forward to keep the inside blade from hitting the boat, forcing the sweeping blade down instead of out. Swing the whole body from the waist to use the full power of the muscles of your torso. It is nearly impossible to roll using only your arms. Think about sweeping out in a broad, level arc with the blade planing along, or just below, the surface. It will support you and lift you toward the surface.

During the sweep your body, which was leaning forward in the set up, is now sweeping around with the paddle adding to its momentum. Your head and torso should follow the paddle's path. You may have to force the situation by holding your head against your arm, or keeping your eye on the blade (a diver's mask will help here). As you start your sweep apply a strong knee lift on the side opposite the side you are sweeping out on.

If all has gone well, as the paddle approaches the straight-out position, the kayak will have rotated halfway up and your body will be at the surface. When the paddle is perpendicular to the boat stop the sweep; beyond this you lose power and can strain muscles. At this point you may need your assistant's help to get back up.

I know this is a lot to remember; in fact you probably won't. Don't worry, in the beginning almost no one does. You'll make mistakes, like sweeping off on the wrong side, but keep trying. Let your helper give you feedback by checking paddle and blade position or even directing the blade through the sweep for the first few times so you can get a feel for the motion.

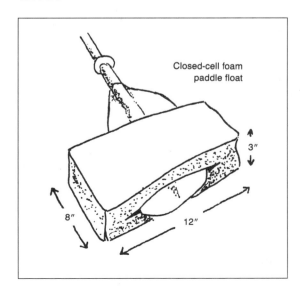

Closed-cell foam paddle float

3"

8"

12"

Practice: Flick and Lay Back

The hip flick used in the Eskimo roll is pretty much the same as any other hip flick, the differences being when and how it's used, and the addition of a sweeping lay back motion.

Have your helper stand in waist-deep water on the side opposite your set-up side. If you set up on *your* left when rightside up, that becomes the *boat's* right when inverted, and the side you'll roll up on. So your helper should be on your right side (yes, it *is* confusing). Place your hands in their proper set-up positions on the shaft. Put the paddle out perpendicular to the boat so your helper can hold the blade near the surface.

Using the paddle for support, lean the kayak over toward your helper and hip flick back up. Start at gentle angles, gradually progressing to going all the way over.

Since the flick and lay back occurs toward the end of the sweep, your head and body are coming up with the kayak and flowing back with the sweep all at the same time. It is important to continue the momentum of both. You will naturally come up as part of the hip flick; but now you have to add that something extra that makes the rolling hip flick different from its generic cousin. You will have to lean backwards as you are rolling up. The progression is: The boat begins to come up, followed by your waist, which is starting to bend toward the rear deck, then your torso, which is swinging up and back, and finally your head, which is almost on the rear deck as the boat becomes level. Not only does this perpetuate the momentum of the sweep, it also lowers your center of gravity and brings the weight of your upper body closer to the kayak's axis of rotation.

You'll know you're getting it if, of course, you can right the kayak. But you'll know you're really getting it if your helper feels a reduction of pressure on the blade. The less pressure on the blade, the more effective your flick and lay back. To further simulate the roll, have your helper hold the blade until you start. He should then take his hands away so you can pull down hard against the water, using only its resistance for support. Once you've got that, it's just a matter of connecting the set up to your flick and lay back with a sweep and you're rolling.

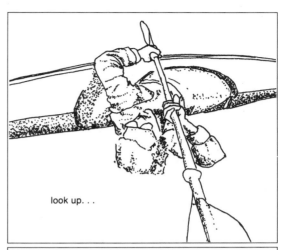

look up. . .

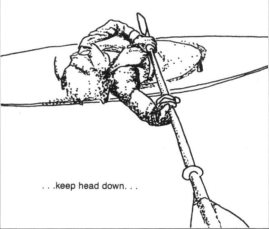

. . .keep head down. . .

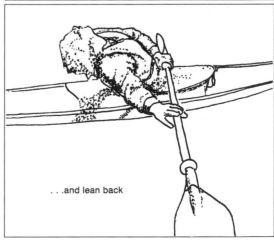

. . .and lean back

ESKIMO ROLL

The Complete Roll

In theory, joining the separate components of the set up, sweep, and flick and lay back should enable you to perform an Eskimo roll. In practice it is not quite that simple or straightforward; but it isn't too far off either.

Although the roll may be divided into separate practice components for the sake of learning, they must not be thought of as segregated movements. The roll should be one fluid motion. It starts with the outward sweep of the paddle and becomes an exaggerated dancer's motion with your body flowing out, around, back, and up. All components are integrated into one forceful drive to the surface.

You'll notice that the series of illustrations begins with the paddler (you) already capsized. How you get there while practicing is your choice. For your first attempts you might want to set up while upright and stay that way while capsizing. Once you are able to roll from this prearranged set up, take it a step further by capsizing while in the paddling position. When you're OK with that, take it to the final stage by capsizing while actually paddling and underway.

After the confusion of an accidental capsize, when it finally sinks in that you're upside down, you must center your thoughts on getting set up. Even in the most tumultuous conditions you'll be able to accomplish this if you do it step-by-step, by the numbers: 1) Paddle over to the side. 2) Hands in place on shaft. 3) Rear hand sets forward blade angle. 4) Forward hand sets shaft angle. 5) Lean forward. To make sure you are set, reach up with both hands to clear the surface, slap the water with the forward blade, and feel for the bottom of the boat with your back hand.

From here it's technique plus determination that will roll you up. While the overall motion must be flowing, it must flow with force. Once you start the sweep, keep going. Put your heart and muscle into it.

Power should come from the muscles of the torso, not your arms. Back this up with a rotating force from the lower hip and knee. The power face of the blade must be facing down and at about a 30-degree angle to assure lift. If you are uncertain of the blade's angle, opt for a little more. Too much may slow down the sweep

and reduce its effectiveness, but at least it won't dive and give you nothing at all.

As in the practice sessions, bring the sweep and your upper body out and around until they are perpendicular to the kayak's side. It is here that you trade the sweeping brace for the downward pull of the high brace. Let your body continue its motion of around, up, and back, while your arms begin to pull down and in. This is the moment of hip snap. Don't try to flick yourself up before this point—it will be futile. When the paddle is at 90 degrees to the boat, hip flick while laying back. Timing is everything.

When it's time to flick up, do it with gusto. Bring your paddle down and past your head with a grand swinging motion. But remember that it's the boat you are flicking up, not yourself. Keep your head in the water until the last possible moment. First, get the boat up, followed by your waist, torso, shoulders, and, last, your head. Do it with an arching back to keep your body as low and close to the rear deck as possible. Stay flexible. Think of your waist as a giant universal joint connecting your hips and the boat to your upper body.

Once up, try to stay that way. Sometimes the momentum that rotated you up can keep you going right around and back over again. There is also a second or two of disorientation upon being upright. In this condition you may need a moment to let your mind catch up to your body. To stabilize yourself keep your paddle in the water and be prepared to make a few short sculling strokes for support.

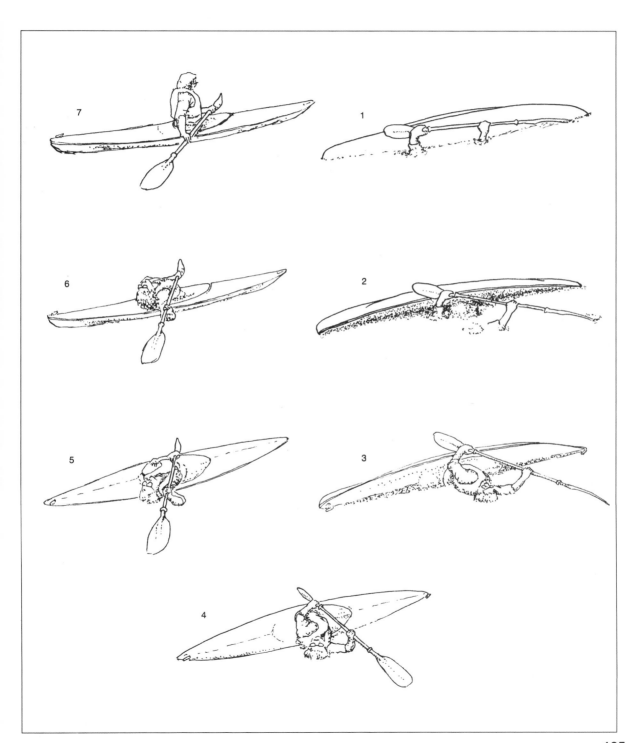

Fine Points

Rolling is an important art to learn, there is no doubting that. But, no matter how proficient you get, don't rely on it as your sole means of recovery from a capsize. Rolling is not an infallible system. Learn and practice at least two alternative methods of self rescue as security backups. Good choices would be the paddle float reentry, and the reenter and roll.

Try not to think of rolling as a panacea, it isn't. In fact it is something that should be avoided. The Eskimo roll is generally the stroke of last resort, an indication that your other skills have failed or have been overwhelmed. Without a doubt it is advantageous to know and practice how to roll. But work even harder at developing a reliable line of defense against capsizing, such as bracing. To paraphrase a well-known kayaking instructor: Mastering the Eskimo roll is a measure of success; having to roll is a measure of defeat. While this is an extreme view, there is some truth behind it. Looked at in a more positive way we could also say that, knowing how to roll is good, but knowing how not to need to roll is better.

Sometimes it can't be avoided, and you are forced to roll because of the conditions you find yourself in. When caught like this your bracing skills may not be up to the job; there are limits. Most often we find ourselves beyond these limits because we've ignored the most primary defense system of all against capsizing—good judgment. Understanding wind, weather, and sea conditions can almost eliminate the risk of a capsize. But sometimes a capsize is unavoidable, unpredictable, or, when caught in the worst of it, thoroughly unbelievable!

If it was wind or waves—as opposed to your own clumsiness—that knocked you over, the rugged situation you left on the surface will be there waiting for you when you roll back up. Be ready to go into a defensive bracing posture when you come back to the surface so it doesn't happen again. There is the well-known anecdote of the kayaker who paddled and rolled (three strokes to every roll) across a particularly nasty patch of water. There's no reason for this paddler to ever be you. Paddling is definitely more fun without having to roll.

The roll shown in this book is a modified screw roll, a compromise between two other rolls: the Pawlata (or extended paddle) and the standard screw, which are all from the same family. Paddle and body movements are similar for all three: You set up, sweep out, and hip flick back up. The main difference is in how the paddle is held.

In the Pawlata roll, named for Hans (or Edi to his friends) Pawlata, the hand grip is very extended. Back then, Edi's idea of rolling was to lever the body and boat up with no thought of using the hip flick. Naturally he wanted the longest lever possible to get the most power, so he grabbed the rear blade by its tip with one hand, placing his forward hand a little behind the center of the shaft. It was like swinging around a long pry bar. It would get you up with a minimum amount of finesse; but your grip on the paddle would be tenuous, making this style of roll slower to perform and shaky in rough water. The Pawlata roll is still used today as a training exercise for beginners wishing to someday graduate to the screw roll.

The screw roll is a good proven general-purpose roll. The best thing about it is that your hands stay in their normal paddling positions. This means there is less confusion in setting up, and more security once you're back on top of the water. Since your leverage is less than for the modified screw, and much less than the Pawlata, good technique is very important to assure the screw roll's success.

As you can see the modified screw roll is somewhere in between these two. It's a good place to start. But if you're having trouble, try the Pawlata roll to at least get you going and feeling like there is a possibility that you might actually roll someday. Work with either style, refine it, and then go on to the screw roll as your final goal.

The more involved you get in sea kayaking, and the further you explore what it has to offer, you will discover that there are a lot more than only these three types of Eskimo rolls. I know of ten offhand, and I'm sure there are more. Some are useful, and some are stunts or of historical interest only. Once you can perform something that at least looks like a roll, study these other types with the goal of defining your own style. In rolling, if it works and works all the time, can be done quickly and safely, it's a good roll.

The advantage of learning with the modified screw roll is that it emphasizes the importance of a solid hip flick and lay back. Which is good, because if there is one thing that could be pointed to as the most common problem area in rolling it would be the hip flick. And within the hip flick the biggest problem is not laying back and having the head come up too early.

The importance of the hip flick is such that if you're good at it you can roll without a paddle. There are stories of Eskimos using broken paddles, harpoons, or knives; some contemporary paddlers can get by using only their hands. This would indicate that whatever it is you are using to sweep out, while important, is secondary to your timing. The sweep merely rotates you up to the point where your body can provide some positive buoyancy. From there on it is the released energy of the hip flick that does the rest.

But even this can be subverted if you succumb to the natural instinct of wanting to get your head out of the water and into the air as soon as possible. Your brace can be strong, but it will be hard pressed to overcome the offset center of gravity of a head and body lifted out of the water. By keeping your head and body in the water their weight is reduced through their own buoyancy (plus that of your PFD), giving your body motion a better chance to get the boat up so you can follow through.

If it is hard to envision or understand the reason for having the boat come up first and not you, think of a falling cat. Cats almost always land on their feet. They do this by righting themselves in mid-air. As they fall they quickly bring their head around so it is level, and then follow through by bringing their body around to line up with the head. You should be doing essentially the same thing with your hip flick. First roll the boat up and then follow through by bringing your body around, allowing the motion of the boat and your hip snap to help pull you up.

The second most common problem area in rolling is the paddle diving as it sweeps around. This can be caused by one of three things.

The first is that the blade angle is incorrect. This is controlled by the position of your rear wrist, which should be locked-in during set up. The second likely culprit is your forward sweeping arm pulling down rather than sweeping out. To avoid this you have to consciously keep your forward arm pushed upward during the sweep to keep the blade on the surface. The last and most probable cause is the improper positioning of your rear arm and hand. Consider this hand as a point that is almost fixed in space, a stationary pivot that moves very little. The paddle sweeps around it while your body is lifted toward it. Hold that arm next to the boat, slightly bent, and high out of the water. Don't let it get pinned against the boat. When this happens you restrict the sweep and cause the paddle to head downward rather than out.

You may not be able to integrate all of this into a functioning roll for quite some time. Learning to roll takes time and thought. You can practice all of these, or any other instructions, perfectly and not get it. Rather than through action, you may be the sort who learns better by thinking things through. In quiet moments try to rehearse the motions of the roll in your mind's eye and play with the mental exercise of envisioning yourself upside down.

One of the obstacles this book was designed to overcome was the scarcity of sea kayaking instructors. If you can, get one. Your life will be much easier for it. But if you can't,

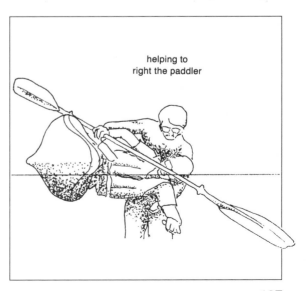

helping to
right the paddler

find a patient, caring soul who will help you through the roll. You'll need him for your own safety and to point out the errors you can't see. While your assistant need not know what a kayak is, he must understand how to right one with you in it. When you are ready to be pulled up give an agreed-upon signal and go into a tight tuck, leaning forward, nose to the deck and arms near the boat. Your helper should be standing to one side. He can then either reach over the bottom or underneath the upturned kayak, grab the far cockpit coaming, gunwale, or your arm, and pull you up and over.

Some words about practicing: Go easy on yourself. Although it takes drive and determination during the stroke, you don't have to carry that attitude over to the whole project. Rest often, and make rolling sessions short to prevent dizzy spells. The human body isn't built for too much of this hanging-upside-down-with-water-in-the-nose stuff. At the least, wear a nose clip to minimize the discomfort. Better still, wear a diving mask to keep the water out and an eye on what you are doing. In the beginning the more input for your soggy, upside down brain the better chances you have of getting this thing right.

If you like, you can make your first attempts at a complete roll using the paddle float. Keep on practicing with the float until you get this assisted roll perfect. At that point you should have a good grasp of what you are doing and why it is happening. From there you have to make the switch over to something closer to a working realty, and start using the paddle without the float.

If you have been paddling with very narrow blades you might want to make the transition from float to bare blade easier by using a wider blade for your rolling. Larger blades provide greater support, which therefore makes rolling easier. In this way you can proceed in gentle steps, going from the float to the large blade and finally to your own paddle. Or you can dive in and try your own right from the start.

Reentry and Roll

Good seamanship is based on back-ups. If one thing doesn't work, have something else in your back pocket ready to go. The Eskimo roll should be your primary means of recovery from a capsize. But, no matter how much you've practiced, something may go wrong and you may not be able to roll up. In a wild predicament fear might paralyze you and affect your ability to react, your rolling skills could be rusty, or a hundred other little things might keep you hanging upside down. When this happens you'll need a back-up. Whatever it is, it should leave you in a more stable position than you were in when you capsized.

One of the better backup recovery schemes is the previously explained paddle float reentry. Not everyone feels comfortable with it, nor is it always possible to use it in extreme conditions. In that case, you'll need another alternative, such as the reentry and roll.

The original reentry and roll technique was concocted to help kayakers who had either tried to roll, failed and exited the boat, or had found themselves somehow washed out of the cockpit. The concept was to keep the boat inverted, reenter as if doing a wet exit in reverse, and then try to roll again. The idea worked in swimming pools but lacked a certain understanding of the realities. (If you couldn't roll in the first place, how were you going to do it the second time, especially after all that mucking about under water?)

Recently the technique has been modified to be more practical and forgiving of your errors, using a paddle float you will now have a much better prospect of rolling up, and having a second chance that really means something.

After capsizing and either failing to roll or purposely exiting the boat, come to the surface. Leave the boat upside down and turn it so it is broadside to the waves with the side you normally set up on as the downwind side. (This is a spatially confusing concept in an inverted boat, worthy of a piece of tape on the set-up side as a permanent reminder.) Get on the downwind side, extract your paddle float from its lashings, and place it on a blade.

Since your PFD will make you too buoyant to get under the boat, rotate the kayak halfway up on its side so you can get in. Your set-up

side should now be above the surface. Face aft and grab both sides of the coaming while holding the paddle on the side you normally would set up on, with the paddle float forward. Now curl your legs in close to the body, get your feet into the cockpit, and pull yourself in. Once you're in, the boat may invert slightly without going all the way over, which is to your benefit. From this halfway-over position you can either try rolling or using a high brace to get yourself all the way up. The choice will depend on how you and your kayak sit in the water.

As soon as you are up, use the paddle float for support by jamming the paddle under the rigging on the rear deck; or, do an over-the-shoulder, one-handed sculling brace. Both of these methods will leave you with at least one hand free to bail and re-seal the spray skirt. If there is proper flotation on board, especially in the form of watertight bulkheads, the accumulated water should be minimal.

Make no mistake about it, the reentry and roll takes practice to master. Putting on a spray skirt with one hand in a rolling sea is nerve-wracking work. But it's worth it if this increases your defensive arsenal.

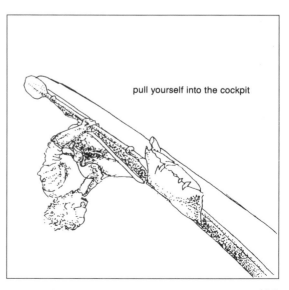

pull yourself into the cockpit

ON YOUR OWN
BUT
NOT ALONE

Two or More

So far everything you have read in this book assumes that you will be on your own. This is not only the most direct method of learning sea kayaking it is also an essential attitude. You are participating in an activity with risks. And whether you are on your own or with others, the risks of your journey are ultimately borne by you and you alone.

As a prudent mariner you must take full responsibility for your actions, and be proficient in and constantly perfecting the basic arts of sea kayaking. You should know how to paddle comfortably and with strength for long periods, be versed in maneuvering your craft, have a feel for balance, keep a well-practiced repertoire of brace strokes, able to Eskimo roll in less than ideal conditions, and know one or more alternate methods of self-rescue. You should understand navigation and weather and be fluent in reading the environment around you. Your vessel is sturdy, well-equipped, fits like a glove, has full flotation, and is supplied with the necessary safety gear. You are properly clothed for paddling or immersion. Even then, with all this, do not be so vain or foolish to believe you are safe. Things you could never imagine will go wrong. Provide backup and contingency plans, to be sure. But in the end the most reliable security will come from having others nearby.

There is that old saying about safety in numbers. Don't believe it for a minute, or doubt it for a second. No matter how big a crowd you have around you, in the end you are on your own; but if you can, never forgo the company of others on the water. It is not that it is unsafe to paddle alone, only much safer if you are not. Once away from land a group becomes a team. A team whose *raison d'etre* is added security, plus (and this should never be discounted) the pleasure and support of companionship in an alien environment.

As soon as someone joins you a team is formed. With a partner along there is help for rescues and aid nearby. But if something really goes wrong it can happen to two as well as to one; or if it only happens to one, the other may not be able to handle it. With three, everyone's chances greatly improve. It is an axiom of life that, while it may take only one person to get into trouble, it usually takes several more to get out. Three boats now offer two to help the one; or, one to help and the other to go for assistance. The odds are improved with three and stay that way until you reach six, with eight being the upper limit. Above this the numbers become unwieldy with too many people to be looked after or to look after others, and smaller sub-groups should be formed.

Once there is a group, of necessity there must then be group management. This is made easier if everyone shares a common goal, is of relatively equal skills, and there is one, and only one, leader. Democracy has never worked at sea, and never will. The leader should not be an all-powerful monarch. He or she is more like the group's mediator, the one person of judgment and experience designated to make a decision in those moments of mass indecision. As much as possible all issues should be discussed and resolved while still on shore. Leaders chosen, routes and meeting or stopping points accepted, communications set and understood, weaknesses and strengths acknowledged. Hardest to deal with will be those group members who go off on their own, reducing the integrity of the team. They are a threat to everyone including themselves.

The logistics of group travel is more clear cut. In launching through surf the leader (chosen for his experience in surf) helps the others out and collects them if something goes wrong. When the others are safely beyond the breakers, the leader joins them. In landing, the order is reversed. The leader heads in and secures the beach, directing the others through the surf. The others come in one at a time watching the leader's hand signals. For example: Arms held vertically means go straight, arms held out to the sides means stop, arms pointing to either side show the preferred direction.

On the water the group can gather in a loose formation. For three boats keep one ahead and two behind, one on each quarter. Larger groups will not stay tightly formed, and the leader is best off to the side or moving freely through the group like a sheep dog. As well as a leader, groups larger than three should have someone ahead, a point man, who is familiar with the route and sets the pace. The strongest or most experienced kayaker should pull up the rear as a sweep to help and encourage weaker paddlers. Within the group, paddlers pair off to keep track and support each other. All paddlers must know the course and cruising plan, but none should set off on his own. To do so subverts the group's security. The point man maintains the course, the rest follow. To add a feeling of equality and variety, and to help morale, responsibilities can be rotated during a cruise. Or, if this all sounds too structured, the group can forget the above and travel as an informal pack. As long as everyone can watch out for each other the results will be the same.

Boat spacing will be difficult to maintain over long stretches of open water. Try to keep boats close enough to communicate but not so close that they cannot maneuver. A good standard is two or three boat lengths between kayaks. Stay within hailing (yelling) distance of each other if at all possible. As it gets rougher close up ranks. Voice communication may be impossible in high winds and visual contact difficult if seas are over three feet as members of the group become hidden in the troughs. In these cases whistles or air horns can be used. A good code is one blast for attention, two for assembly, and three in case of emergency. Hand signals similar to those used for surf landings can also be used. When one paddler sees the signal of another, that paddler should also signal. Thus the message gets relayed quickly throughout the group. Signals must be kept simple and easily understood. At night, both sound and light signals can be used.

Group decisions should be based on the performance of the least experienced or weakest paddler. This can be frustrating to the more advanced but should be upheld. Do not encourage the less experienced to push their limits just so they will not hold you back. To do so invites disaster. Ideally everyone in the group should be capable of rescuing others and be responsible for his own emergency, navigation, and rescue gear as well. Discuss and, if possible, rehearse rescue procedures before leaving.

When emergencies such as a capsize or gear breakage occurs the two closest boats should assist while the others standby, holding their positions nearby but not so close as to add to the problem. The group should stay together during these emergencies and not be tempted to disperse.

A good way of holding your position while not underway is by rafting up. Rafting is an ideal method of resting, eating, making repairs, or coming close to discuss matters without having to continually paddle to hold your position. To raft, come abreast of another kayak so you are both facing in the same direction and bridge the two boats with your paddles. In this way the two kayaks become a wide, flexible, and very stable single vessel (raft). More boats can be added to the raft as desired.

Groups, as well as the lone traveler, can add an extra measure of safety to their trip by notifying a responsible person on shore of the proposed cruise. This "float plan" should include time of departure, expected route, stopping points, final destination, and time of arrival. Tell a friend or on longer trips the Coast Guard. The procedure is to check in when you've arrived; if no one hears from you, a search along your known route is initiated.

Without a doubt it is safer to cruise in a group, but never be lulled into a false sense of security just because you are surrounded by others. While they can help, stand by you, and get you through situations that you might not have been able to cope with on your own, you should still, in the end, consider yourself to be responsible for your own actions.

Assisted Rescues

There are two types of situations where even the most experienced solitary paddlers will not be able to rescue themselves. One is when they can no longer propel their craft; the other, being the worst of all circumstances, is when they have become separated from their kayak while far from shore. Neither is an admirable position to be in and both absolutely require outside assistance.

Someday you or someone you are with may become unable to continue under his own power. Paddles break, wrists go out, people get sea sick, exhausted, or weakened by exposure. It can be any number of things. But if your boat, or a boat that is with you, has been properly set up for towing, the predicament need not become a disaster. What is necessary is a bow line rigged, or a special line stowed, and ready for this purpose.

The disabled kayak will most likely be drifting broadside to the wind. Approach from the windward side to set up the tow line. The line attached to the towing boat must be done in such a way that it can easily be made secure, immediately freed, and will not foul deck gear. A quick-release fitting (such as a cam cleat), can be permanently bolted in place behind and off to one side of the cockpit. An alternative is for the towing paddler to hold the rope. One way is to tie a bowline in the end of the tow line and put one arm through the loop so it rests over your shoulder. To get free, let go of the paddle on that side and let the line slip down your arm. To make life a little easier keep the tow line two or three boat lengths long, especially in following seas, with one boat length as a minimum.

Worse than not being able to continue on your own is to find yourself separated from your boat. It is probably the most demoralizing situation anyone could find himself in. Even a small lake becomes ominously large, the ex-paddler dwarfed and defenseless. It has been sadly recorded how drowning victims believed that shore looked closer than it actually was. If your kayak has gone down or been blown away, don't try to swim for it. Immediately signal your comrades for help.

The first priority is to get the swimmer out of the water to reduce the risk of exposure (hypothermia) which is the greatest disabler and killer of kayakers. The rescuing kayak should turn into the wind and hold its position. The swimmer then drags himself onto the aft deck, staying face down, as low as possible, with legs spread for stability, holding on to the waist of the paddler. For short distances, such as bringing the swimmer to his kayak or a nearby shore, the swimmer can hang off the bow with legs and arms wrapped around the hull, head off to one side.

Swimmer rescues and towing can and should be practiced. Emergencies will always throw in the unexpected, and no one technique or method will always work.

Assisted Reentry

Nothing is quite so desperate as a lone paddler swimming next to his capsized kayak. Even in calm conditions the feeling of being totally cut off is demoralizing enough to induce panic; at a time like this having the support of others becomes invaluable. You may have your paddle float reentry down pat and have practiced rolling until you're dizzy, but one day it may all fall apart and your only recourse will be an assisted reentry.

Upon finding yourself in the water after a failed roll or some other disaster, an assisted reentry will be much faster than trying to do it on your own. Climbing back on board while somebody steadies the kayak makes it more likely that you will be able to get yourself together and on your way with less hassle or wasted effort. In most cases the assisted reentry is the most reliable rescue there is. But, as with everything else, you should know the drill and have practiced it before it's ever needed so a capsize and subsequent rescue becomes only a minor annoyance, not high drama at sea.

Upon being called over to help, get to the downed kayaker as soon as possible. The preferred set up is to be on the windward side of the boat with both bows pointing in the same direction. But don't waste too much time maneuvering about. If it's faster to be on their downwind side with the boats pointing in opposite directions, do it. This procedure will work either way.

When the two boats are together the person in the water should right his kayak. Do not bother bailing it out just yet. Take both paddles and lay them across the boats directly behind the cockpits. Or, if the boats are pointing in opposite directions, place the paddles behind the coaming of the rescuing boat and in front of the coaming of the boat being rescued. The rescuing kayaker then leans over, puts his closest arm under the paddles, between the boats, and reaches forward to grab the other boat's coaming. The paddle shafts are now trapped under the rescuer's armpit and pressing down on both decks. The rescuer's weight is on the paddles, not on his arms. The forward hand can be used to steady the boats by holding the other's coaming or, since that hand is not bear-

ing any weight, held out to help the paddler being rescued.

The person in the water stays even with his cockpit, grabs hold of the extending paddles with one hand, the coaming of his kayak with the other, and pulls himself onto the aft deck facing astern. Staying as low as possible, with most of his weight towards the rescuing boat and the rescuer counterbalancing any movements, he works his legs into the cockpit, turns over, and slithers down onto the seat. Once in, the rescuing kayaker should continue holding on until the one being rescued has bailed his boat, re-secured the spray skirt, and feels ready to go it on his own.

A modification to the above is to use a continuous loop of rope or nylon webbing as a sling to help get back in. It is more than likely that part of the reason you wound up in the water was because you were too tired to react properly. While the standard assisted reentry is easier than a self-rescue, it still takes a goodly amount of effort to haul yourself up and into the boat, an effort you might not be capable of. A sling eases that job by letting you use your more powerful leg muscles to push, rather than only using your arms to pull.

The sling is wrapped around the cockpit coaming and is long enough to hang off the side like a stirrup just below the bottom of the boat. You then put one foot in the sling and push yourself up onto the kayak. Slings must be accurately measured, tied ahead of time, and stowed away in a spot that will be convenient to reach when you are in the water.

A final word about rescues: There may come a time when conditions are so bad, the sea so raucous, and the wind so blinding that the best way to save anyone is by *not* trying to rescue them. Your only hope being a signal for help and the belief in higher intervention. But I know that this will never happen to you because, through good judgment and seamanship, you will not let yourself get into that sort of desperate situation in the first place.

THROUGH THE SURF

Launching

Avoid surf as much as you can. If it is at all possible, and most of the time it is, plan your journeys so they begin and end in sheltered water. When paddling on bays, creeks, and smaller lakes this should pose no problem. But on larger lakes, or when cruising an ocean's outer coast, you may have no choice.

Given the proper equipment and some experience, kayaking in surf can be a lot of fun. In a highly maneuverable, slalom white water or specialized surfing kayak, you can play with abandon (almost) in the breakers. But sea kayaks are not built for this kind of stuff. They like to go straight and are reluctant to turn, traits that are to your advantage once out in the open, but within the surfline can mean some occasional excitement. If you can't avoid paddling through surf, or are perversely drawn to it, at least make sure your sea kayak is strongly built, has rugged foot braces, carries no deck cargo, is fitted with carrying toggles (not loops) at both ends, and has 100-percent failproof flotation.

If you have to deal with surf, try to arrange things so you only encounter it on the way out. Going out through surf is a lot easier and safer than coming back through it. For one, you know exactly what you are getting into. When sitting beyond the surfline contemplating a landing all you see are the backs of the breakers, but from shore you see the whole show. You are therefore afforded the luxury of going out or staying put, rather than being offshore and having no choice at all in the matter.

To put things more in your favor look for waves that spill rather than curl and collapse on themselves; they have less punch. In very general terms there are two kinds of breakers: spilling, which break with foam cascading down their face; and curling, which curl over and dump their tops at the base. Seek out a beach with spilling waves, products of a gently sloping bottom. These usually break away from the shore in multiple surflines with a lot of broken water (soup) between them and the beach. Curling waves are caused by bottoms that drop off or shelve steeply and generally break closer to shore in a single surfline.

If you've decided to head out, spend some time studying the surf from a high vantage point. Know what you are getting yourself into. Check the beach at low tide to see if anything lies beneath the surface, like rocks, coral, or steep drop-offs that could make things difficult. Notice how the surf breaks at both tides, one is usually better than the other. Be aware of the direction and strength of the wind. Strong offshore (coming from the land) winds hold waves up to delay breaking or can even flatten them completely. Sea breezes push a messy chop ahead of them, generally increasing throughout the day, and becoming still near dawn.

Take your time to look for patterns in the surf. You may find sections that, because of bottom contours, break differently from others. Rip currents, outward bound streams of up to five knots, flatten waves and can be used for a free ride. You'll observe that the larger waves come in sets or a definable pattern. To decipher this pattern you may be able to count the waves or time the period between sets. Neither will be absolutely accurate. Your best bet is to remember the pattern, recognizing how high the largest look and what comes before and after them. Get a feel for the surf. Try to envision a window of opportunity where the waves are at their least powerful, with more green than white water inside the breakline. The idea is to launch and be nearing the line after the largest wave of the set has spent itself. Be patient and wait.

Know the size of the waves you will encounter, with anything over six feet as your limit. You can judge heights by standing at water's edge. If the top of a breaking wave extends over the horizon line, it is higher than your eye level. Do the same for smaller waves by standing on your knees (about 4 feet) or sitting (about 2 1/2 feet). This is a reasonably accurate method, although waves somehow seem to be a lot larger when looming overhead.

To launch, place the kayak in the shallows or on the beach where the wash from larger breakers can reach it. Point it directly into the waves. Get in and seal yourself up. If you are on the beach, wait until the surge reaches you, push down, and hand walk your way in until you are afloat. This may take a few waves to do. When able to paddle, keep the bow pointed into the waves until you've built up some forward motion. If a small bit of soup grabs the bow obliquely before you are underway, it can swing the boat around, making it difficult, if not impossible, to get pointed back in the right direction. Whenever you have a helper let him give you a shove straight out or hold the bow until there's a lull and you can get going.

Once free of the beach, paddle with force and determination. Use short brisk strokes so you can react quickly to balance or alter direction. Your course is head on at right angles to the waves. Don't rush the first few strokes. As you paddle out try to pace yourself by holding back or sprinting to miss the worst of it. If you've timed it right, and are lucky, you'll be able to get outside the breakline without a major confrontation. As a wave approaches, whether it is broken white water or is still a swell, you'll get over it as long as you keep paddling. When it arrives lean back to help lift the bow and then forward as it passes; all the time aggressively paddling to attack the wave, clawing your way over.

There will be times when you're not so lucky, and you'll see that the wave is about to break right on you. If it is small, under three feet, keep your head down with chin buried in your PFD. Time your strokes so that when the wave hits the bow a blade will be entering the solid part of the wave. As the wave reaches you, pull yourself through, letting the PFD take the impact. Do not stop paddling or hold the paddle up with the idea that the wave will pass around you. It will, but it will also wash you backwards or smash the paddle's shaft rudely back into you. Paddle through with force. If the wave is steep, you'll come flying out the back like a Polaris missile. It's a great rush and perfectly permissible to whoop like mad while in flight.

If you've miscalculated the surf from the shore and are about to be pounded by something with genuine malicious intent, your response will have to become equally virulent. When faced with a towering monster dig in and paddle like someone possessed (with the will to live). The attack plan is to build up maximum momentum so you will punch right through the wave. Keep your head down, so the water has less to grip on, and your weight forward. It is most important to avoid being hit in the upper body by the full force of the wave which has the potential to drive you back or over and back. Paddle on no matter what. As you emerge from the wave's back congratulate yourself, take a deep breath, and continue on with all haste out of the surfline. Keep up a steady pace until you are further out than you would think necessary, otherwise a large set may come through taking you by surprise.

If you've really miscalculated the size and power of the surf, you may have to adopt a more defensive tactic. When surfers think they are going to get creamed by a wave they flip over and let the bottom of the board take the brunt of it, while their bodies create enough drag to keep them from being swept back in. If the wave is less than six feet high and you have a failproof roll, you can do the same. Set up for the roll, capsize, keep your head well tucked in towards the deck for protection, hang in there while it feels you are going through the rinse cycle, and when the wave has passed, roll up. Back on the surface paddle like crazy to get out of the line of breakers. You should only have to roll once on the way out.

Capsizing to protect yourself from curling breakers can be dangerous. In fact being in curling surf isn't too wise to start with. There is a very real possibility of being flipped over backwards and tossed around as if in a cocktail shaker. In these extreme situations your only defense may be to capsize the boat, get out of it, and hold on to the bow toggle. In this way you will slowly be dragged back towards the beach to rethink your options.

Landing

When standing offshore confronted by a breaking inlet, prudent mariners from time immemorial have taken one of two approaches: go elsewhere or wait. Only the uninitiated, over-confident, or impatient would charge blindly into the breach, ignoring the precepts of discretion and sound judgment. It is no different for sea kayakers sitting beyond the surf, wondering what to do.

If you are thinking of landing through surf, consider option number one and go elsewhere. In most cases surf is something that can be avoided. Plan ahead. Look for coves, points that stick out to create protected beaches, sheltering rocks, small islands, or a passage that bypasses the outer shore altogether.

Option number two, waiting it out, is almost impossible for a kayaker. Wind and waves take a long time to change.

But if there is absolutely nowhere else to go, and the surf looks or sounds threatening, you may have no choice.

When it can't be avoided, you'll have to chance it and head in. If you've estimated the waves to be no more than six feet with a good landing spot on the beach, there is no reason why you shouldn't make it. Your first task is to learn what's waiting for you inside the breakline. Check your chart for bottom contours, see if the beach is sand or rocks, or if there are any off-lying obstructions. Stay away from swimmers. Once it is ascertained that you've found a likely spot, wait. Sit well outside the surfline and feel how close together the waves are, their speed, height, and steepness. Larger waves break further out. Find where they break and paddle near. If it doesn't seem too bad, start looking for a pattern.

Waves conveniently organize themselves in sets, multiple wave systems superimposed upon each other as they near the shore. When the troughs of these patterns coincide you get a lull, when the peaks come together the surf becomes larger. Sets can be tracked by counting, by timing, or by simply remembering their pattern. You want to come in on the small ones which follow right after the largest waves of the set.

Your best plan of attack is not to be picked up by a wave and have it hurl you shoreward.

Surfing may be fun, but once underway you relinquish almost all command of your craft. To maintain some semblance of control you want to paddle in under your own power, close behind and on the back of a breaking wave.

It is a matter of timing. After you are positive that the last large wave has passed, paddle in towards shore where the smaller waves will break. Stay outside this breakline. As a small one comes in paddle backwards to prevent taking off as you feel the stern lift. When the stern starts to drop the wave is passing and you should begin paddling for all you're worth. You want to be high up on the back of the wave so it will carry you along as it breaks in front of you. Do not get ahead of it or you'll go over the falls and start surfing. Don't lag too far behind or the counter current on its back will hold you, with the chance of being overtaken by the next breaker.

Since your very best paddling speed is probably five knots, and the wave is traveling at double (or triple) that, you won't be able to hold on to one wave all the way in. Try to get through the main line of breakers. Once in the soup you can surf in or paddle with an occasional back stroke as a holding action.

Another method of getting in under control is to come in backwards. This technique gives you an out anytime you find things are not going well, making it perfect for landing on unknown beaches. However it is not suitable for large surf (over six feet) or surf that breaks right on the shore.

Start by paddling in on the back of the last large wave of a set. Get in as far as you can

Follow in on the back of a wave.

and turn seaward before the next wave reaches you. If it is breaking, paddle towards it so you won't be swept backwards. The larger the breaker, the harder you'll have to paddle to maintain your position. Between waves paddle backwards towards the beach. Like a boxer you can bob, weave, parry, and thrust, maneuvering your way shoreward in safety. Do not use your rudder during this type of surf work. It is too vulnerable and easily broken or bent if bounced along the bottom. Stick to the basics of paddling for steering.

If the breaker is small enough, and you're willing to forgo some control for a little adventure, you can surf in. Wait for a wave and paddle before it. Unless the surf is very small (under two feet) do not head straight in. Hard-to-turn boats, like sea kayaks, have a tendency to rush down the wave's face and bury their noses (pearling). The wave then grabs the stern and slews it around (broaching); or in big waves you can wind up standing on end (appropriately called an endo) with your stern in the air and the unlikely chance of coming down rightside up.

As you gather speed lean back to keep the bow up and slow yourself down. Using a stern rudder on the side you wish to turn towards, head diagonally across the face of the wave. If you can, steer away from the white water where the wave has already broken. Since you are no longer on level water, lean in towards the wave to keep your balance. Leaning away from a wave will guarantee a capsize. If the wave is very steep, convert your stern rudder to a low brace and lean on that. Eventually the part of the wave you are on will break. There will be a surge of power shoreward which must be counteracted by aggressively leaning towards the wave, supported by either a high or low brace depending on the wave's height. As you are swept along in this controlled broach keep your arms close to the body and flexible to absorb the considerable buffeting. On smaller waves plant the blade on the wave's back. When you can't reach over the wave, stick the paddle high up in the soup. You'll get a surprising amount of support, but little control over where you are going.

If you capsize, immediately lean forward and tuck in to protect your head. If you can, try to roll up. If you can't, get out of the kayak as soon as possible. Whether you've left the kayak on purpose or were washed out by a wave, your first objectives are to keep the boat upside down so it doesn't fill and to stay seaward of the kayak so it doesn't get thrown into you. If the surf is moderate, you can hold onto an end of the kayak and let the waves push you in. Hold only the kayak itself or a toggle. Do not put your hand or fingers in a grab loop. A kayak rolling in the surf can make these into twisting nooses that can entrap you. If the surf is not so moderate, get clear of the kayak as quickly as you can and swim in with the paddle.

Once you reach the shallows get out and carry the boat above the waterline. In surf that breaks close to, or directly on, the shore get the boat up on land as fast as possible before the backwash sucks it back out. While holding the boat in the wash keep it end-on to the oncoming waves, otherwise you'll be chasing it up and down the beach with banged up shins.

Bracing on a breaking wave.

The Controlled Broach

1

2

3

4

WIND AND WAVES

Into

On its own, wind is not much of a problem for sea kayaks. Its primary effect is felt in how the boat wants to situate itself in relation to the wind. This is weathercocking and each boat is different. Fortunately most kayaks want to point their bows into the wind while underway, making it very easy to paddle in that direction.

Waves are not so benign. Like big goons, they are there to do wind's bidding. It takes time to get them going but, after being pushed by the wind for a while, they begin to follow in its direction. The longer they're pushed, the meaner they get. Unless you kayak in a seismographically active area almost all the waves you'll confront will have been born from the wind. This could mean a wind that is ten miles away, or a thousand. Each wave is a composite, with its size determined by how long and hard the wind has been blowing, and how far it has traveled.

While waves are products of the bullying wind, they are also easily manipulated by others. Any current from either a river or a tide running against the wave pattern will cause them to steepen. Shallow underwater ledges or irregularities confuse them, narrow funnelling passages hasten them, points of land can bend them, and steep shorelines or bulkheads can bounce them around. Because of the diminutive size of our vessels even small wave patterns can be a challenge. But the contest is not one sided. Given the proven seaworthiness of a skillfully handled sea kayak you can come out on top if you go at it with an aggressive attitude. Attack waves. Lean into and push towards them. By taking the offensive you can often bully them right back.

If you are paddling into the wind when there is little wave buildup, your main problem will be stamina, having enough strength to keep going. Paddling into a strong wind can easily cut two or more knots from your speed. At a cruising speed of three to four knots, losing two is a major setback. All you can do is resolve yourself to it and keep moving as fast as you can. Find a paddling rhythm with a strong stroke that can be maintained and dig in. Put full body twist into it and push with the recovering arm. Lean forward to reduce windage and get weight to the bow to forestall any

possibility of being momentarily blown off course. Ease your stroke during gusts, paddling with just enough pressure to keep the boat moving.

How much wind is too much? In protected waters where waves are not a significant factor, a beginner should have no trouble in winds up to twelve miles per hour. From twenty miles per hour on, even protected bodies of water will be effected by the wind and should be left for more experienced kayakers. Somewhere around thirty miles per hour is the maximum limit for almost everyone, with progress into it bordering on impossible.

On open water the game changes as waves become part of the equation. In light winds the waves are just enough to make paddling interesting. Your kayak will feel alive, there's some spray flying, and the waves rushing towards you make it feel as if you are going much faster than you are. As the wind picks up so will the waves. On smaller swells, time your strokes so the paddle enters an oncoming wave and begin pulling back as the crest arrives. On larger waves, paddle hard on the downward slope and ease off on the upward slope. Widely-spaced, deep-water swells are easiest, as they gently undulate past. More troublesome is the short chop found in shallow waters that have recently been whipped up. These short period waves can make the boat plough in, which can be alleviated by shifting your load or leaning back to lighten the bow. Turning in waves is difficult and is best done on wave tops. This gets the boat's ends out of the water, making it easier to effect the turn.

Paddling into wind and waves forces you to expend a great deal of energy on propulsion, yet a minimum on balancing. Going to windward may be hard work, but it has the advantage of being the least vulnerable course because it is much harder for a wave to knock you end over end than it is to roll you over on your side. Also, waves are psychologically less threatening if you can see them coming, rather than having them sneak up astern or abeam. When things get out of control, or you need to take a break, head into the wind and hold your position with a slow, forward stroke. This is the rough water way of putting the boat in neutral.

Across

Sea kayaks are at their most awkward when wind or waves are coming from their sides. It's part of their nature; something that can't be avoided, but can be dealt with.

With the wind on your beam the kayak's desire to weathercock can become a demanding nuisance. Very few, if any, are neutrally balanced to the wind. Almost all want to veer off in one direction or the other, and to varying degrees. For safety reasons, most boats, if they weathercock at all, do so to windward. This means that the further away from paddling directly into the wind your course takes you, the more you will have to compensate for weathercocking.

In gentle winds, carved turning may be sufficient to hold your course without sacrificing forward speed. By tilting the boat toward the wind it will tend to head downwind. Plus, with the boat on an angle, your stroke automatically becomes wider on the lower (windward) side, helping to keep the bow away from the wind. If this isn't having the desired effect, the next step is to broaden the sweep of your stroke. If that doesn't do it, shift your grip a few inches up the shaft to increase your leverage on the sweeping side.

Another way of handling weathercocking is to alter the boat's underwater profile by adding more area aft. If your boat is equipped with one, lowering the skeg will help balance its steering and may prevent the stern from swinging downwind and the bow from pointing up. If you have a rudder, try doing the same by keeping it centered. As the wind increases you will have to begin compensating with the rudder. You'll find that as long as you are moving the rudder need only be turned a few degrees to neutralize the most severe weathercocking. Your paddling style and rhythm will not be affected and good progress can be made.

As the wind gets stronger, keep your arms and stroke lower. This increases the bracing component of the stroke and prevents a gust from getting hold of the windward blade on its return stroke (more likely with a feathered than a non-feathered paddle). If the wind hits your blade and wants to carry it away, don't fight it. Release your grip on the windward side and let the paddle go where it may. Holding on can put

you off balance and increase the chance of capsizing. Just let it go, bringing it back at a lower shaft angle to resume paddling with some extra caution.

As the wind builds so will the waves, increasing the probability of being knocked over. To the edging (tilting the kayak) that you are already doing for the carved turn, you will now have to add some leaning (tilting the body) to help counteract the lateral capsizing potential of the waves and to resist the wind. As when paddling into the waves, here too you have to take an aggressive stance and always lean toward them. The larger and steeper they are, the more you have to lean. Do this by adding a bracing blade angle to your stroke for support and forward propulsion, without letting it hinder your cadence.

The only thing that should interrupt your pace are waves so large or steep that they become threatening. Your only defense will be to break stride and brace as you did while surfing. Depending on the wave's size, go into a high or low brace. As the wave hits, lean into it and sustain the brace until it passes. Another tactic is to turn into the big ones so you take them bow on. This only works if you can turn your boat easily and quickly, which may be difficult in a beam sea. If a few forward sweeps on the downwind side won't turn you, try three or four reverse sweep strokes on the windward side. These may slow the boat down but offer a more powerful turning force. You may find it impossible to turn your boat when it is in a trough with the ends trapped between two waves. If so, wait until the boat rises to the top of a wave, reducing its immersed length, then try to turn.

While all this is going on, and you're concentrating on just making forward progress in the right direction without losing your balance, you are simultaneously being blown sideways with the wind. Make allowances for this drift. Line up two points to act as a reference to see just how much you are drifting off course.

With

Finally! Here's a course where you can lighten up and let the wind do some of the work, right? Well, yes, but it's not quite that simple.

When the wind is light, under ten or fifteen miles per hour, your only concern may be some mild weathercocking. If you are heading exactly in the direction of the wind, it won't have any effect other than to push you along your way. But as soon as you let the wind get even the slightest bit to one side, it's going to try to swing you around. When this happens it should take only minor course-correcting strokes to keep you headed in the right direction. A forward sweep stroke ending in a stern rudder should do it. Just don't let the boat yaw too far off course before making your correction.

The deceiving part about downwind travel is that because you are moving with it the wind never seems as strong as it really is. But there's always that moment of surprise when you stop, or turn into it, and find that what you thought was a nice cruising breeze is, in fact, a nasty blow. Keep an eye on the waves. If they have grown to the point where you have to fight to keep from broaching, you've let things go too far.

Before that, as the waves are building, you will find yourself hitching rides and gaining ground with each wave. At this stage they have grown to where their internal motion alternately pushes you ahead and holds you back. The water particles in the crests move with the wave and those in the troughs against it. To use this to your advantage, paddle a little faster as your stern lifts to the oncoming wave. When you feel

yourself accelerating, paddle even harder. If the waves are the right size, you may even surf for a short distance. As the crest passes and your bow lifts, the forward push is over. Once in the trough, strong paddling will do you no good, so stroke only to keep from being drawn back. As the next wave approaches the cycle starts over again. In this manner your progress will increase with a noticeable decrease in effort. Get attuned to the wave pattern so there is no need to put yourself off balance by continually looking over your shoulder to see what's coming. Feel what the waves are doing and let yourself go with them.

As wind and waves build you may find your downwave speeds increasing at an alarming rate. These rapid accelerations are akin to surfing, with all its inherent dangers. Your main concern now is not making progress but retaining control. After you have been picked up by a wave and are running with it, use a stern rudder stroke to manage direction, being ready to convert it into a low brace if you veer too far off and begin to broach. When you feel you are no longer in total control, or frequently come close to broaching, it is time to stop surfing and begin slowing down. To reduce the likelihood of taking off stop paddling as the wave builds up behind you. Or, you can back paddle to act as a brake, letting the crests pass by completely. Although you may feel you are lagging behind by doing this, you are still being blown downwind and making reasonable time. An alternative for really big swells is to turn into it and let yourself be blown backwards while holding your bow to the wind and waves.

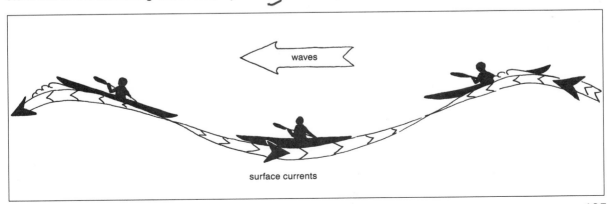

waves

surface currents

Electives:

EXPANDING YOUR HORIZONS

Weather

Sea kayakers are slaves to the weather. No other water sport is so dominated by it. White water kayakers couldn't care less if there is a strong crosswind or that their river is shrouded in mist. But sea kayakers faced with a wind on their beam know that they'll be in for a day of fighting to keep on course, and fog means lost navigational landmarks or being surprised by fast-moving power boats. Even sailboats aren't as affected as kayaks. Size alone lets them overcome obstacles that would stop a kayak dead.

The scale of a sea kayak to its environment makes it that much more sensitive to what goes on around it. Next time you're paddling with someone spend a moment to watch how his boat goes through the water. If you can, let your imagination go for a second and you'll see a scaled-down ship on scaled-down waves. Remember those films from World War II where you'd see a destroyer or some other sleek warship pushing through the seas of the North Atlantic? Well, seen through a reducing glass, kayaks are in the very same position. A sea kayak is but a tiny ship to which a three-foot wave is analogous to a giant North Atlantic roller.

Sea kayakers are not only interested in the weather in general but the weather in very specific locales. Micro weather patterns as well as macro need to be understood.

For us, weather is very area specific. Sitting in a kayak, your horizon is two miles away. That's your world. The weather contained within it is what should concern you most. General forecasts, even good, accurate ones direct from the weather service, are of only moderate use. These are good for getting a hint about broad patterns, but they are often made up of data collected fifty to seventy-five miles away, which for the highly localized world of the sea kayaker make them almost irrelevant. Consider your own experiences. How many times have you heard a weather report and wondered if they had bothered to look out the window? It's not their fault. It's just that, for example, wind velocity and direction are bound to be different if they are collected in downtown Miami than only five miles away on open Biscayne Bay. So you've got to learn how to interpret both the general patterns of weather and, more importantly, what is coming at you from the horizon, your immediate weather patterns.

For collecting general weather information your best sources are the dedicated weather channels on VHF/FM radio frequencies and the weather report on your local TV news program. The radio forecasts can be picked up on marine VHF/FM receivers, the weather band on multiband radios, or inexpensive specialty radios that only receive the weather. All these radios have frequencies pre-set to get exclusive recordings from local weather stations affiliated with the National Oceanic and Atmospheric Administration (NOAA) in the U.S. and the Coast Guard in Canada. These frequencies are designated as channels WX-1, WX-2, WX-3 in the U.S., with an additional WX-4 in Canada. Each channel broadcasts weather from a different local weather station. Depending on where you are and your radio's strength, you will get in different channels and reports from different weather stations. Each station also includes reports from individual Coast Guard and automated facilities within its area. In this way you can build up a fair image of the general weather pattern.

To do this you must be able to understand the language of these reports. When they say that winds are light and variable it means that the wind has a speed of five mph or less and varies in direction. A Small Craft Advisory means winds of twenty-five to thirty-five mph, and a Gale Warning is for winds from thirty-five to fifty-five mph. Beyond this, ratings should be of only academic interest to the sea kayaker.

If you acquire information more easily when it is presented visually, try the local TV weather forecasts. While the forecast itself may be as useless as the "weather person" announcing it, what is valuable are the niceties that they throw in. Most helpful are the radar pictures of weather at that exact moment and an up-to-the-minute weather map. Radar is a wonderful thing in that it shows where concentrated cells of bad weather are located and in what direction they are moving, all within a relatively small sector.

When you are completely out of touch with any of these electronic marvels you'll have to depend on your own observations to forecast general weather patterns. For the untutored in meteorology this could be an almost impossible task. But if you can tell which direction the wind is coming from and read a barometer, you can make some surprisingly accurate forecasts using the tables that follow.

These tables represent a composite of long-term observations for weather behavior throughout most of the continental U.S. and lower Canada. Its reliability diminishes below 30 degrees and above 50 degrees north latitude. There is nothing mysterious about it and, with a little studying of basic weather, you'll see that it directly relates to typical patterns associated with areas of high and low pressures. These pressure changes are measured by a barometer which should be consulted every three hours during the day to ascertain pressure trends. Barometers can be conveniently carried with you in the form of a compact combination altimeter/barometer, available through camping or mountaineering supply sources.

There may be times when it seems that you have nothing at all to guide your forecasts. No radio, TV, barometer, or tables. When this happens you will have to depend on your own capabilities. Even if you don't know an isobar from a juice bar, it's easy to do if you are willing to let yourself tune in and really see what's around you.

Noticing your surroundings is not difficult in a kayak, and is often what people find that they like about the sport. Moving at three mph inches away from the water's surface and repeating a simple relaxing motion for long periods, paddlers have plenty of time to absorb what is going on around them. In your daily routine the patterns and effects of the atmosphere are there, but often seem inconsequential or go unnoticed altogether. Once you come in direct contact with the world, as you do in a kayak, you get closer to feeling the environment as our predecessors did.

Not too many generations ago there were no "official" weather reports, and people looked around them, heard, felt, or saw signs that they could read as nature's weather reports. These got handed down as folk sayings: some quite fanciful, others based on hard facts of empirically gained knowledge. This stuff is for real, and it's only recently that the United States Department of Agriculture stopped publishing one of its oldest pamphlets on folklore and weather. So, when you seem to be without anything to guide your forecasts, try looking around for some of these ancient indicators of weather.

- The most famous bit of weatherlore is one of proven worth and was spoken by Christ in Matthew 16:2,3. "When it is evening, ye say it will be fair weather: for the sky is red. And in the morning, it will be foul weather today: for the sky is red and lowering." The old red sky at night sailor's delight, works. Most weather travels from west to east. If the setting sun were seen through the dust of dry air, it would appear red and fair, dry weather would arrive the next day. Makes sense. Here are some other signs to look for.

- If you wake up to find that there is dew, it will be a fair day, while a dry morning is a sign of rain. This is because the heat absorbed by an object during the previous day can only be released as dew or frost when the night and early morning is calm, clear, and cool.

- Rain can be foretold by the phenomenon of far-off shorelines seeming closer than usual. When this happens rain is usually less than a day away. During fair weather a great deal of salt haze evaporates and is held in the air. The mixing action of unstable pre-storm air clears this away, visibility improves, and objects seem closer.

- A halo around the moon is another sign of rain. The halo is caused by the moon shining through ice crystals of moisture-laden clouds. If the halo is a tight fit, rain is still far off. If the halo forms a large ring, rain is near. If the clouds set in and the moon loses its outline, rain can be expected in about ten hours. The same is also true with the sun.

- When smoke from a ship's funnel curls downward and hangs by the surface it means approaching rain. This is caused by the lowering air pressure which precedes rain. Since the air is not dense enough to support the heavier particles in the exhaust

Wind and Air Pressure Weather Forecaster

By entering in the wind as you observe it, and the trend of the barometer for the preceding three hours, you can arrive at a fair estimate of the coming weather. This chart is intended for use in continental North America between 30 and 50 degrees north latitude. Barometric readings are in inches of mercury.

WIND	BAROMETER	FORECAST
SW to NW	30.1 to 30.2, steady	Fair with slight temperature changes for 24 to 48 hours
SW to NW	30.1 to 30.2, rising rapidly	Fair followed by rain within 48 hours
SW to NW	30.2 and above, stationary	Continued fair with no major temperature changes
SW to NW	30.2 and above, falling slowly	Slowly rising temperature and fair for 48 hours
S to SE	30.1 to 30.2, falling slowly	Rain within 24 hours
S to SE	30.1 to 30.2, falling rapidly	Increasing wind and rain within 12 to 24 hours
SE to NE	30.1 to 30.2, falling slowly	Rain within 12 to 18 hours
SE to NE	30.1 to 30.2, falling rapidly	Increasing wind and rain within 12 hours
E to NE	30.1 and above, falling slowly	Summer: If winds are light, no rain for several days Winter: Rain with 24 hours
E to NE	30.1 and above, falling fast	Summer: Rain probably within 12 hours Winter: Rain or snow with increasing winds
SE to NE	30.0 or below, falling slowly	Rain will continue for 24 to 48 hours
SE to NE	30.0 or below, falling rapidly	Rain with high winds followed within 36 hours by clearing and colder in the winter
S to SW	30.0 or below, rising slowly	Clearing in a few hours and fair for several days
S to E	29.8 or below, falling rapidly	Severe storm imminent, followed by clearing within 24 hours and colder in winter
E to N	29.8 or below, falling rapidly	Summer: Severe NE gale and heavy rains Winter: Heavy snow and cold wave
Going to W	29.8 or below, rising rapidly	Clearing and colder in the winter

it lingers near the water. Another sign of rain is that a boat's engine exhaust, horn, or any other loud sound, will have a hollow clarity as if heard down a tunnel. This is caused by a lowering of the cloud ceiling so sounds bounce back; in fair weather the clouds are too high to do this.

- Some old sailors insisted that they could smell an oncoming rain. This makes sense because the lowering air pressure allows previously captive odors to escape. Notice how much more ripe seaweed and low tide muck smells before a rain. You may also notice that if the air is moist, and the air pressure already low, that rain will most frequently come at low tide. This is nothing more than the air pressure being further reduced by the lowering of the water's level.

- When the weather is fair it can be expected to stay that way if the bases of the clouds are high or you see a rainbow to windward. When weather is foul and the wind begins to veer, clear weather is on the way. Wind is said to change its direction by either veering or backing. A wind that veers is changing its direction to your right as you face it. This is a sign of a clockwise wind common to high pressure areas which bring clear, fair weather. A counterclockwise wind is from an area of low pressure which brings a promise of foul weather. "A veering wind will clear the sky; a backing wind says storms are nigh."

- All winds have personalities dependent on their direction. Each is surprisingly unique. The west wind, because it travels over land, traditionally brings fair dry weather. This, of course, is not so on the Pacific coast or Gulf coast of Florida where it often brings rain. West winds prevail in the U.S. and are reversed most often by the presence of an area of low pressure. This brings an east wind with cloudiness, a drop in air pressure, and a rise in humidity. From Izaak Walton's 1664 fishing classic *The Compleat Angler:* "When the wind is in the west, there it is the very best. But when the wind is in the east, 'tis neither good for man nor beast." When winds from the north and south encounter the prevailing westerlies, or each other, the

colliding air masses can trigger all sorts of havoc, usually in the form of precipitation. The north brings snow and the south rain.

The most frightening sort of wind for the sea kayaker is anything that comes up fast. At an all out speed of six mph you're not about to out-run anything. So when the prospect of a thunderstorm or line squall looms on your horizon you better have a good idea of what it is going to do to get the maximum amount of time for a defensive action.

The line squall is the edge of a cold front. Whether on the bridge of a battleship or in a kayak, it is one of nature's most impressive shows with the front pushing ahead a boiling, tearing, sulphurous yellow and black cloud with a turbulence that can be heard. As it hits, the wind shifts and comes bowling down at speeds of more than fifty mph. There's thunder, lightning, rain, and a noticeable chill in the air. And then it's over.

Luckily squalls, or any rains associated with a cold front, go as fast as they come, supporting the saying that "The sharper the blast the sooner it's past." Another lucky point is that they are completely predictable. Any lightning or storm clouds seen in the west or northwest will most likely reach you, but those seen to your south or southeast will pass. If it looks like you are going to get hit, you should prepare yourself for the oncoming winds. To know how the wind will shift, face into the pre-storm wind. The wind will shift to your right after the storm has passed. Just before this shift, when you are right under the black squall clouds that act as the storm's messenger, you might experience a lull or a wind blowing towards the storm. After these clouds go by and a few heavy rain drops fall, the sky may lighten a little, tricking you into thinking that it is over, and then wham! You get blasted by the front itself with heavy rains, lightning, and a cold wind from a new direction. But in a few minutes it's all over; leaving the world and you soaked, shaken, and now bathed in cool, dry air.

Another fearsome yet fast moving terror are the thunderstorms. These can happen on their own, independent of a cold front, created by the upwelling of moist air that has been heated

Wind Speeds

mph (knots)	Pressure in pounds/ square foot	Description	Wave pattern	Probable wave heights	Effects on land	Kayaking conditions
1—3 (1—3)	.004—.04	Light airs	Glassy calm, some ripples	Flat	Flag hangs limp, smoke rises vertically	Beginner
4—7 (4—6)	.06—.20	Light breeze	Overall ripple pattern	0—1/2 foot	Flag stirs, leaves rustle, wind felt on face	Beginner
8—12 (7—10)	.25—.58	Gentle breeze	Small glassy waves	1/2 —1 foot	Flag occasionally extends, leaves and twigs in constant motion	Bginner— intermediate
13—18 (11—16)	.68—1.30	Moderate breeze	Longer waves	1—1 1/2 feet	Flag flaps, small branches move, dust and paper raised	Intermediate
19—24 (17—21)	1.44—2.30	Fresh breeze	Some whitecaps	1 1/2—2 1/2 feet	Flag ripples, small leafy trees begin to sway	Intermediate— experienced
25—31 (22—27)	2.50—3.84	Strong breeze	Regular pattern of whitecaps, some spray	2 1/2—4 feet	Flag snaps, larger branches in motion, whistling in wires	Experienced only
32—38 (28—33)	4.10—5.78	Moderate gale	Swells form with whitecaps	4—5 1/2 feet	Flag fully extended, whole trees in motion, resistence to walking	Extremely difficult for experienced
39—46 (34—40)	6.08—8.46	Fresh gale	Foam blown off wavetops in well marked streaks	5 1/2—7 1/2 feet	Twigs and small branches broken off, difficult to walk	Impossible to paddle into
47—54 (41—47)	8.84—11.66	Strong gale	Waves begin to heighten and roll	7 1/2—10 feet	Structural damage occurs	Survival conditions
55—63 (48—55)	12.10—15.87	Whole gale	Very high, rolling waves with long over-hanging crests	10—13 feet	Trees broken or uprooted, considerable structural damage	Your life flashes before you

Notes: Wind pressure varies greatly according to the shape of an object. Pressures shown are only approximate. Wave patterns are described for large, open lakes or oceans. Smaller bodies of water will have diminished wave patterns. Also, wave patterns will be different near abrupt shore features, like cliffs, or when the wind is blowing against a current.

during the day. While they can strike at any hour they most often occur in the late afternoon or early evening. Signs to look for are singular, dark cloud formations of great height, terminating in an anvil-shaped top that points in the direction of travel. As with a line squall, there is a preceding line of low, rolling clouds. But with thunderstorms these clouds bring a violent shifting of winds from an updraft, then a brief lull followed by even more violent down drafts, thunder, and rain as the first clouds pass. The down-drafts continue, always blowing out towards the edge of the storm, until the storm has passed over.

Besides wind, line squalls and thunderstorms also bring lightning. The only good thing about lightning is that it can tell you how far off the storm is, which translates into how much time you've got to get under cover. Base your calculations on sound traveling at about a fifth of a mile per second. After you see a flash, start counting the seconds until you hear the thunder. Multiply the number of seconds by one-fifth (0.2) and you get the distance. Sometimes you will see something commonly called heat lightning, where you see the flash but do not hear the thunder. This is because it is too far off for the sound to reach you. But it is not too far off to make its presence known as static on an AM radio, which is an excellent, early warning system for storms.

While the intensity of the line squall or thunderstorm is impressive, it is short-lived. On a day-to-day basis prevailing winds are the most important element of weather concerning the sea kayaker. Beyond certain extremes, temperature is of little consequence. You step outside, see how it feels, and dress accordingly. The likelihood of a sudden change in temperature, say 20 to 30 degrees, is highly unlikely. Precipitation, while it can be uncomfortable or limit visibility, shouldn't hold you back. But wind, if you're not careful, is what will do you in.

The wind's speed and direction are very difficult to predict, even for so-called experts. Sailors have been trying with limited success for centuries. So don't knock yourself out doing what can't be done. The one thing you can do though is to know what you are dealing with at

the moment. Standing on the shore you should be able to judge what you will be getting yourself into. For every course relative to the wind, and every kayaker's abilities, there are winds which will be too much and winds that will be beneficial. You must be able to judge which you will be faced with by sight and by feel.

The wind speed chart on the previous page offers a variety of indicators from which to assess the speed of the wind. The exact speed, or the speed expressed as a number value, is unimportant. What is important is understanding how a specific amount of wind will affect you on the water. Whether you know this wind by how a flag flies, tree shakes, or the way it stirs the waves is immaterial. As long as you know the potential of what you will encounter.

The only value of knowing the wind's actual speed is in the ability this gives you to understand the increasing forces. The force (pounds per square foot of pressure) that a wind exerts is exponential to its speed. That is, when the wind speed is doubled, its force is squared. For example, if the wind doubles in speed from five to ten knots, its force quadruples. A little wind goes a long way, and a little more goes even further.

All of what has been said here is an attempt to make your paddling more enjoyable and safer by giving you some inkling of how to predict the weather. In all fairness, and any honest meteorologist would agree with this, no matter how prepared or educated you are in these matters there's always an element of chance.

Disabled Paddlers

"Many people have told me that when I'm in my kayak I don't look handicapped. Well, in my boat I am not handicapped. I am still disabled—I have physical limitations, but a handicap is a disadvantage, a barrier, that prevents a person from doing something. Steps leading to a building handicap me. But when I am in my boat, I am free to focus on the beauty of the world around me; and my body, which is so uncooperative on land, is part of the sleek craft gliding through the water." Janet Zeller, disabled sea kayaker.

Almost 25 percent of the American population has some sort of physical disability. That's a tremendously high number, one in every four persons; so there's a good chance of your being that one in four. If you are, you may feel held back and kept from sampling the full quality of life. But if deep within you there is a desire to get out on the water, if you believe that that is what will make your life better, then there is no need to hold back any longer.

You've probably heard it said that those with disabilities have enough difficulties to overcome, why add to them with a sport that may contribute further risks and discomfort? The reason, of course, stems from those very same difficulties that are reducing your participation in life. They are why you, as a disabled person, should pursue an activity like sea kayaking. There's no need to put aside your love for the outdoors or adventure. Nor is there any reason for you to be denied the pure fun and sense of accomplishment that comes from paddling.

The sea kayak is an ideal and almost universal vehicle for those who are willing to try it. For someone who is confined to a wheelchair it can be a great equalizer. Think of it like this: The human body is not built for or capable of traveling over the water on its own; in this sense all humans are to some degree handicapped. To overcome this handicap kayaks were created to sit in while arms are used to move about; just as a person on land uses a wheelchair. This artificial device for transportation on the water, the kayak, is an equalizer.

Your body, which may resist your wishes on land, becomes part of a vessel when in a kayak, that is more at home in its element than any other. You are literally a part of the boat and the water that supports it. On the water there is freedom, all the barriers that land presents to a wheelchair, or any other device, are gone. It is just you and the unrestricting water.

In sea kayaking the disabled paddler need not be thought of as such, in most cases being able to participate on a par with the able-bodied paddler. Unlike other sports which have been adapted by the physically disabled as parallel activities, sea kayaking lets you act and be reacted to as an equal to all others. Because there are more similarities than differences between able-bodied and disabled paddlers, it is your ability, not your disability, that determines with whom you paddle. You are less isolated from the rest of the world, and can share experiences with little or no concessions to your handicap. Also, sea kayaking offers its own benefits in that it is highly therapeutic, building upper body strength and extending ranges of mobility.

Evaluating Your Abilities

There are many types of disabilities, each with its own restrictions; most can be adapted to the minimal limitations of a sea kayak. The hearing impaired, blind, those with lower limb handicaps, amputees, or someone recovering from a heart attack are all potential kayakers. It is something done in a seated position with as little, or as much, energy expended as the participant feels comfortable with. In the end, it always comes down to a personal challenge: Are you really physically capable of kayaking? If there is even the slightest temptation to try it, it's worth taking the chance to find out.

Most lower limb handicaps are surmountable for kayaking. More difficult, but still possible, are conditions like cerebral palsy, spina bifida, muscular dystrophy, polio, multiple sclerosis, cystic fibrosis, or spinal cord paralysis. Individuals with these handicaps will have to evaluate their own abilities. The same situation exists for those with diabetes, arthritis, asthma, Down's syndrome, stomas, or epilepsy. If the risks are considered acceptable, there is nothing holding you back. Sensory disabilities, like hearing or visual impairment, vary in severity; but even the most severe cases can be overcome by paddling in groups or in double boats. The mentally disabled may also participate. You will have to judge for yourself: are you comfortable and confident in the water? Will the logistics of transportation, getting in, out, and using the kayak be too overwhelming? Are you willing to put in the work to achieve the goal?

More than likely if you are prepared to make the effort, you can probably become a competent sea kayaker. But where to start? Paradoxically you will have to begin at two places. You will need an instructor and you will need to choose and adapt your equipment.

To a large extent your equipment will be determined by your disability. Clothes may be particularly important if your handicap is affected by cold or heat. Usually there is a need for extra warmth or protection. The choice of using a neoprene wet suit may not be the right solution for you. Neoprene is difficult to get on and off and does not lend itself well to special tailoring for non-standard proportions. Instead you might want to try one of the many thermal pile fabrics. While not as good an insulator in water, pile is far superior in air and considerably more comfortable and less restrictive. Doffing and donning can be facilitated by simple alterations and closures made of easily handled Velcro. If bruising is a problem, localized padding can be added.

Everyone, able or disabled, should wear a PFD. The problem with most is that they are not made to accommodate special needs. Making any changes to a Coast Guard certified flotation device technically voids its approval, but when it comes down to it, you may have no choice in the matter. Many find that the standard PFD is too hard to put on or take off and rides up in the water. A simple improvement is to add a large, easy to grip tab on the zipper slide. Waist straps can be secured with velcro for easy adjusting and crotch straps can be sewn in place to keep the jacket from riding up.

When choosing a PFD make sure that

there is enough room and adjustments to go over extra layers of clothing. You'll find that ones made of solid slabs, rather than narrow panels, are a little more confining but do provide extra rigidity for your back. If needed, extra back support could additionally be built into the jacket by stitching or just sliding in a foam pad. PFDs can also provide extra insulation and flotation by using a Class I rather than the usual Class III jacket.

Spray skirts can present a daunting problem to handicapped paddlers who find themselves inverted. While they do keep you warmer and drier, they also make exiting more difficult. To help, make the release cords more obvious and easier to grab hold of. If that does not solve the problem you may have to sacrifice some watertightness and fasten the skirt to the coaming with Velcro. The skirt will then be easier to jettison, while still keeping most of the water out.

Your choice of kayak and paddle will be even more complicated than for an able-bodied paddler. Everyone's parameters will be different. Depending on your handicap extra support and padding may have to be fitted, paddles modified, and many small details worked out for your personal needs. If you are visually impaired or have limited upper body strength, you may need a double kayak and the help of another paddler. Whatever it is, most problems can be accommodated. It's the premise of flexibility, something for everyone at their own pace, that makes sea kayaking so accessible.

The level of your disability will determine the amount of adapting necessary. Don't get carried away with your modifications. The more complicated anything gets, the more likely it is that something will go wrong. Keep it simple, strong, foolproof, and test everything first in controlled conditions before venturing out.

If you have lower limb disabilities you might want to consider a more stable boat, one that is wider or has a flatter bottom. Adapting the kayak will most likely be necessary because control of the boat is accomplished through the lower body, which must in some way be secured in place. Like other paddlers you must wear your boat. Most work will have to be done in the seating area. You may have to redesign

the seat itself by adding extra padding or back support. Ethafoam or Ensulite are excellent materials for this. Even if you have lost torso stability, the seat back can be extended or wrapped around to increase support so you can transfer upper body motion to the kayak. Back straps and seat belts, although controversial, have been successfully used when incorporating appropriate quick release buckles such as found on jet ski straps. Take cockpit size into account for ease of entering and safety in exiting. You might want to consider a double (two person) boat if you cannot manage a single on your own.

Before adapting a paddle, consider the choices of already available equipment. Try a longer than normal paddle for more stability and more efficient turning for weak paddlers or to extend the reach of paddlers with limited use of their arms. A lighter paddle may be desirable and is always easier to handle. Small blade areas require less effort and have less impact on muscles and joints. Consider non-feathered paddles if you have wrist or hand disabilities.

Some adaptations are very simple. If you are weaker on one side than the other, shift your grip closer to the blade on the stronger side. For those with poor vision you may need an index on the shaft so you can feel the blade's angle. This can be done by wrapping tape around any object that is thick enough to provide a raised indicator. Shafts can be made thicker or narrower to suit your grip.

Other problems take a bit of engineering. If your grip is weak, a glove with velcro on the palm can be used to make contact with velcro on the shaft. Retaining straps can be designed to hold hands in place. Any variety of creative solutions are possible. For those wearing a prosthesis there are manufactured, waterproof terminal devices specifically design to hold a paddle. There are compasses with Braille faces and waterproof hearing aids. The solutions are out there. But you'll more than likely find that the adaptations within you are more important than those you make to your equipment. Although your body may be limited in function, it is your positive attitude, not a gadget, that will overcome most of the obstacles.

Once you have the equipment adapted the

work begins. You must now learn to paddle and stay safe. Everyone has the right to take risks, that is how growth proceeds, but it is foolish if they are unnecessary. Learn to paddle properly with an instructor. Of all the resources available to you, your instructor will be the most valuable. Do not try to learn on your own.

Instructions for a disabled paddler are usually just about the same as for anyone else. All paddlers should feel at ease in the water with and without a PFD. It is not absolutely essential that you be a good swimmer, but if you are a non- or weak swimmer, it is worthwhile to take classes before proceeding. After that, learning the basic skills should not be too much different than for anyone else.

The one area you might have to work harder on is self-rescues. Some creative thinking may be necessary for wet exiting, finding ways of getting back in a capsized boat, or generating enough hip snap to accomplish an Eskimo roll. Experimentation, practice, help of others, and a good instructor will be your best assurances of success.

More than the learning process, the biggest challenge of sea kayaking for the disabled is making the decision to start. Once you get going you'll be pleasantly surprised at how quickly you progress. Set your goals realistically, building slowly to more advanced situations and techniques. Make it as tough or as easy as you like for you are challenging yourself, not an opponent or anything else, which is what makes sea kayaking so rewarding.

Sea Kayaking Access

Over the past few years people with special needs have become much more organized. The result has been that opportunities are now available for anyone to lead a more satisfying life with increased access to the world. In the U.S. the best place to start is:

American Canoe Association
Disabled Paddlers Committee
Box 1190
Newington, VA 22122-1190
(703) 550-7495

The association works with paddlers, would-be paddlers, therapists, and instructors; acting as a clearinghouse for information.

Other organizations are:

Challenge Alaska
Box 110065
Anchorage, AL 99511
(907) 563-2658

Environmental Traveling Companions (ETC)
Fort Mason Center
Landmark Bldg. C
San Francisco, CA 94123
(415) 474-7662

Maui Sea Kayaking
Box 106
Puunene, HI 96784
(808) 572-6299

Nantahala Outdoor Center
US 19W
Box 41
Bryson City, NC 28713
(704) 488-2175

Pacific Water Sports
16205 Pacific Highway S.
Seattle, WA 98188
(206) 246-9385

Shared Adventures, Inc.
76 Eastland Ave.
Rochester, NY 14618
(716) 442-8104

Shared Outdoor Adventure Recreation (SOAR)
Box 14583
Portland, OR 97214
(503) 238-1613

Vinland National Center
3675 Ihduhapi Rd.
Box 308
Loretto, MN 55357
(612) 479-3555

Wilderness Inquiry
1313 Fifth St., SE
Suite 327 A
Minneapolis, MN 55414
(612) 379-3858

Books for the Disabled Paddler

Canoeing and Kayaking for Persons with Physical Disabilities, American Canoe Association, Box 1190, Newington, VA 22122

A Guide to Canoeing with Disabled Persons, British Canoe Union, Mapperley Hall, Lucknow Ave., Nottingham, NG3 5FA, England

International Directory of Recreation Oriented Assistive Devices, Life Boat Press, Box 11782, Marina del Rey, CA 90295

Introduction to Kayaking for Persons with Disabilities, by John Galland. Available from Vinland National Center, 3675 Ihduhapi Rd., Box 308, Loretto, MN 55357

Resource Manual on Canoeing for the Disabled, Canadian Recreational Canoeing Association, Box 500, Hyde Park, Ontario, N0M 1Z0 Canada

Family Kayaking

Kayaks are made for families. Of course the word families is an obvious euphemism for kids. So let's just say kayaks are made for kids, which they are.

The Eskimos encouraged their children to play in kayaks from about five years on; at the age of six or seven they would be taught to paddle, and by twelve they were learning to roll. All kids, whether they're brought up on whale blubber or Whoppers, have a remarkable sense of balance and movement. Starting them early is a good idea. They are more flexible, have fewer pre-set notions of what should or should not be, have smaller egos, are willing to make mistakes in order to learn, and actually learn faster than most adults. Give them some instruction, let them try, and they'll be paddling before you know it.

Where to start? Begin with yourself and master the basics. You're going to have to know what you are doing in order to teach your kids; in addition, you have no right risking their safety by not being adequately trained. When to start? Probably yesterday. The earlier the better, within reason, that is.

Infants make notoriously poor paddlers; but they do enjoy being held or nestled between the legs of a passenger in a triple or, for short distances, by the forward paddler in a double. It's awkward but it can be done. Your primary worry will be safety. Since no commercial PFDs are available that small, some homemade device will have to be created, preferably one with a grab handle on the upper back. Clothing is vitally important at this age. Because of their small body mass, young children are prime candidates for hypothermia. They cool down very quickly, and must be kept warmer than you might think. Don't dress them to suit your idea of the temperature. You're going to be paddling and burning energy, they'll be just sitting and getting a chill. So bundle them up.

For everyone involved it is always best to dress in layers. In warm weather keep cotton underpants next to children's skin to absorb perspiration. In colder weather dress them in fishnet underwear to trap body heat and wick away moisture. A covering layer should be added as an insulator which can be modified as the weather changes. For infants their main fashion statement will be diapers. With older children it can be anything; but on camping trips they'll need more clothes than an adult, at least a full change per day for kids up to twelve. They'll need rain gear, too. Ponchos are fine and cheap enough to be replaced when ripped or lost.

The next age group, preschoolers from one to five years, are perhaps the most difficult to deal with. They are too large to hold, too young to paddle, too old to sleep for very long, and get bored easily. For long trips they may not be the best company as they require an incredible amount of specialized care and gear. At this age they start to become aware of things, which is wonderful; and insist on making some of their own decisions, which can be frustrating.

If you hope to get them into kayaking, it is here that you will have to work to make it a fun experience, something they'll look forward to doing again. On a cruise this may not be the easiest thing to do because they are at the height of their I'm thirsty, I'm hungry, I'm tired, I'm bored, I have to go to the bathroom phase. The best pacifier is to go by their schedule not yours. Keep trips short with a lot of diversions. If that isn't enough, snack food will usually hold a fidgety kid from insanity (and you from murder) for a while. Patience and seeing things through their eyes is the key to success. Show them what's out there. Put them in touch with the world beyond TV. You'll find that how a kid relates to the wild is usually entertaining and often quite bizarre. If you can, get them to slow down and see. Show them the wonders of a tide pool or the secret life of ducks. It doesn't have to be exotic. Once they learn to see, they'll love it and the real adventure will start.

A triple cockpit boat may be your best bet. The center cockpit can be fitted out as a cosy floating playpen with special attention paid to padding and safety. If a triple is not available, a single's rear hatch can be used. This is good only for short distances because you can not keep an eye on the child and they cannot stay in eye contact with you.

You might be better off when they are this age to postpone longer trips for awhile and get them started playing in and around kayaks, so there are fewer fears when it comes time for

their first lessons. Purposely upset the kayak with all aboard as a game, letting the kids get used to what happens. Give them time to swim and play on and around the boat until it becomes a friendly environment. Make sure

they have their own equipment. There's nothing like having your very own Snoopy PFD with a neat emergency whistle attached to make a kid feel like he's part of it, while at the same time building good safety habits. This is also a good

time to enroll kids in swimming classes. A kid in a proper fitting PFD with secure crotch straps to keep it in place may not need to know how to swim, but one who is at home in the water and not threatened by it may help keep a life-threatening situation from becoming a panicky emergency. Whatever you do, make it fun and don't push it.

Once a child is old enough for grade school, from six years to their early teens, they are old enough to try paddling their own smaller boat or pulling their own weight for short distances in a double. If you'd like your child to get interested in kayaking this is the age to do it.

After early adolescence it may be too late to instill new disciplines. The grip of peer pressure, rebellion angst, and hyperactive hormones all make it unlikely that you'll have a happy, first-time kayaker on your hands.

By starting kids young, families can be bonded by kayaking. But it has to be done carefully. Kayaking is not something the typical kid decides he wants to go out and try. Children have to be introduced to it slowly and in small doses. Two to three hours is the maximum attention and fidget-free span, so don't just paddle around. Go hide under docks, watch birds, picnic at a nearby beach; whatever you do it must be fun. Once kayaking and fun become synonymous, they'll be hooked and ready for longer trips and more learning.

Put them to work right away. Lack of physical activity gets kids antsy. Let them "paddle" right from the start but, also, let them decide when not to. A single-blade paddle if they're in the middle hatch of a triple, or a small, double blade if they're forward in a double may be best. Get them their own equipment and make sure it's right. A good paddle is just as important for them as it is for you. When you think they're up to it, get them their own boat. At this writing the only children's sea kayak being made is by Northstar Kayak & Canoe Co.

Don't underestimate kids' ability to adjust, just give them space, security, and input; you'll be surprised at what they can do. Let them keep lookout, "navigate," and help to plan the route. Always let them actively participate in what's going on. But remember, they are still

kids and need their own special support systems. On long trips they'll need their toys, security blankets, teddy bears, books, and your binoculars. Plus, they'll need unusually large amounts of bandages, bug repellent, and toilet paper.

Sometimes it is hard but parents must not be obsessively goal-oriented when on a cruise. Getting to where you set out for may be your goal but it more than likely is not the kid's. The objective of a kid is to have fun and that means fun in his own way. You are going to have to accept the idea of a diversion-centered trip. You've got to go with the flow. Stop and look, picnic and go for a walk, fish, anything to keep it new and interesting. Your challenge is to control the environment while offering progressively more demanding opportunities without over-extending limits of confidence and competence. Think of it as a controlled adventure.

Finally, keep photo records of whatever you do. Weeks later the things that were so horrible look funny in photos and often make kids ready to try it again. They also make neat stuff for show and tell.

If you are lucky enough to have a kayak-loving teenager, the adolescent years can be the most rewarding. The contemporary teenager seems to be bombarded with all sorts of unnatural stresses, and sea kayaking can be the perfect escape. For kids who are non-athletic it lets them get outdoors and taste adventure without having to compete. The kayak teaches independence, self-esteem, accomplishment, responsibility, and gives something that's just different enough to be interesting without being too "weird." Kayaking is also great for incorporating other interests like photography, fishing, snorkeling, or a little amateur marine biology.

The bottom line is that sea kayaking is meant to be enjoyed. With some preparation and careful attention to how you approach it, paddling with kids can actually be fun. It can also be rewarding, is definitely inexpensive, frequently relaxing, almost always brings a family together, and might even be worth putting up with the occasional "are we there yet?"

Appendix

Periodicals

ANorAK, 34 East Queens Way, Hampton, VA 23669. A loose network of sea kayakers who exchange tips, information, ideas, and names. Published bi-monthly.

Canoe, Box 3146, Kirkland, WA 98083. Some sea kayaking articles. Best for its annual Buyer's Guide in December as a comprehensive listing of sources.

Messing about in Boats, 29 Burley St., Wenham, MA 01984. Frequent sea kayaking articles. Great source of used boats. Published twice a month.

Paddle Sports, 1509 Seabright Ave., Suite B-1, Santa Cruz, CA 95062. All kinds of paddling in all kinds of boats. Published quarterly.

Sea Kayaker, 6327 Seaview Ave. NW, Seattle, WA 98107. The only magazine dedicated to the sport. Published quarterly.

Books

Advanced First Aid Afloat, by Peter F. Eastman. Everything from amputations to zits.

Alone At Sea, by Hannes Lindemann. Atlantic crossing in a folding kayak. A great adventure, if not literature.

The Ashley Book of Knots, by Clifford W. Ashley, 1944. Over 3,800 knots and their practical usage for everyone from kayaker to tree surgeon. Encyclopedic and practical.

At The Sea's Edge, by William T. Fox, 1983. An introduction to coastal oceanography for the amateur naturalist and terminally curious.

The Audubon Society Nature Guides. Guide book series for the Atlantic and Gulf coasts, and the Pacific coast. Animals, plants, and geography of the regions.

Baidarka, by George Dyson, 1986. History of the Aleut Eskimo, Russian fur traders, and their mutual effect on the local evolution of the kayak and the author.

The Bark Canoes and Skin Boats of North America, by Edwin Adney & Howard Chapelle, 1964. Development of these craft by Native Americans. Good historical information on Eskimo rolling.

Canoes and Kayaks for the Backyard Builder, by Skip Snaith, 1988. Tack and tape method of building some good-looking and inexpensive boats from plywood. Plans for a 16-footer and 18-footer.

Cockleshell Heroes, by Cecil Phillips, 1957. British kayak forces behind enemy lines in WW II. Good show!

Cooking On The Go, by Janet Groene, 1980. 300 recipes for those with no refrigerator, oven, broiler, grocery store, or Cuisinart.

Dangerous Marine Animals, by Bruce W. Halstead, 1980. How to avoid all those nasty things down there.

Derek C. Hutchinson's Guide to Sea Kayaking, by Derek Hutchinson, 1985. A seasoned kayaker's manual of esoteric information with a biased point of view.

Dictionary of Fishes, by Rube Allyn, 11th edition. Best field guide for identifying those with whom we share the water.

Eskimo Life, by Fridtjof Nansen, 1893. Contemporary observations of traditional kayaks, kayaking, and way of life for Greenland Eskimos.

Eskimo Rolling, by Derek Hutchinson, 1988. Everything you ever wanted to know, or thought there was to know, about the subject.

Finding Your Way On Land or Sea, by Harold Gatty, 1958. When everything else fails there's navigation by observing nature through sight, sound, and smell.

Foldboat Holidays, by J. Kissner, 1945. Interesting period piece about boats in a bag and the paddlers who were beginning to sense their potential.

Fundamentals of Kayak Navigation, by David Burch. Seat of the pants navigation for those with wet seats. Very complete and practical.

The Heroes, by Ronald McKie, 1960. Desperate escape from the Japanese by Australian commandos in kayaks.

How To Survive On Land or Sea, by Frank C. Craighead, 1984. The classic book on survival. Great if that's what you're into, or need.

Kayak Cookery, by Linda Daniel, 1987. Camping and cooking for touring sea kayakers.

Kayaks Down the Nile, by John Goddard, 1979. Down to the sea in folding kayaks.

Kayaks to the Arctic, by E. B. Nickerson, 1967. One family's story of How We Spent Our Summer Vacation. Theirs was in the Arctic.

Keep It Moving, by Valerie Fons, 1986. A 2,400 mile endurance run down the Baja coast. The paddling never stops.

The Klutz Book of Knots, by John Cassidy. Connect the dots type instructions for 25 basic knots. Book includes 5 feet of rope.

An L. Francis Herreshoff Reader, by L. Francis Herreshoff, 1978. Worth it for one chapter, The Dry Breakers, telling of a contemplative paddle out to, and night spent on, a barren patch of rocks.

Navigation Rules: International and Inland, by the United States Coast Guard, latest edition. Required reading for those who paddle in populated waters. Rights of way; plus sound, light, and day signals.

Oceanography and Seamanship, by William G. Van Dorn, 1974. An encyclopedic work on wind, waves, currents, and how they affect things afloat.

On the River, by Walter Teller. Anthology of some of the best writings from the turn of the century about cruising in canoes and kayaks.

Piloting, Seamanship and Small Boat Handling, by Charles F. Chapman. Since 1922, this frequently-updated text has been the bible for power and sail boating, with most of the material equally applicable to the sea kayaker.

Qajaq, by David W. Zimmerly. Readable and beautifully presented historical research into the kayaks of the north Pacific.

Rushton and His Times in American Canoeing, by Atwood Manley, 1968. The growth of paddling sports in the U.S. in the 19th century.

Sea Kayaking: A Manual For Long Distance Touring, by John Dowd, 2nd edition. A seasoned kayaker's manual of slightly less esoteric information with a slightly less biased point of view.

Sea Touring: An Informative Manual for Sea Canoeists, by J. J. Ramwell, 1980. Published under the aegis of the British Canoe Union, dedicated to producing polished paddlers in a country that insists on calling kayaks canoes.

Seekers Of The Horizon, edited by Will Nordby, 1989. Excerpts from writings by sea kayakers about their journeys out and, sometimes, back.

The Starship and the Canoe, by Kenneth Brower, 1973. Multilevel true story about an eccentric Northwest kayak builder and his rocket scientist father.

Wood and Canvas Kayak Building, by George Putz, 1990. Complete plans on how to build, plus advice on how to use and maintain, a 17-foot and 18-foot kayak.

Gatherings

During the year sea kayakers come together at symposia, festivals, workshops, etc., for their common benefit. Listed below are only a few of these. For more, and updated, information contact: Trade Association of Sea Kayaking (TASK), Box 84144, Seattle, WA 98124, (206) 621-1018.

Advanced Coastal Kayaking Workshop. Contact: L. L. Bean, Inc., Freeport, ME 04033

Alaska Pacific University Kayak Symposium. Contact: Alaska Pacific University, 4101 University Dr., Anchorage, AK 99508

Angel Island Festival & Regatta. Contact: Sea Trek Ocean Kayaking Center, Liberty Ship Way, Sausalito, CA 94965

Atlantic Coast Sea Kayaking Symposium. Contact: L. L. Bean, Inc., Freeport, ME 04033

East Coast Sea Kayaking Symposium (Charleston, SC). Contact: TASK, Box 84144, Seattle, WA 98124

Great Lakes Kayak Touring Symposium. Contact: Great River Outfitters, 3721 Shallow Brook, Bloomfield Hills, MI 48013

Hornby Island Kayaker's Festival. Contact: Hornby Paddling Partners, RR 1, Hornby Island, BC, Canada V0R 1Z0

Inland Sea Kayaking Symposium. Contact: Trek & Trail, Box 906, Bayfield, WI 54814

Jersey Shore Sea Kayaking & Bay Canoeing Show. Contact: Ocean County Dept. of Parks, Lakewood, NJ 08701

Mystic Sea Kayaking Symposium. Contact: Mystic Valley Bikes, 26 Williams Ave., Mystic, CT 06355

West Coast Sea Kayaking Symposium. Contact: TASK, Box 84144, Seattle, WA 98124

West Michigan Coastal Kayaking Symposium. Contact: Lumbertown Canoe & Kayak Specialties, 1822 Oak Ave., North Muskegon, MI 49445

Kayaks

Alaskan Kayaks, SR-1, Box 2425, Chugiak, AK 99567

Aquaterra, Box 8002, Easley, SC 29640

Baldwin Boat Co., RFD 2, Box 268, Orrington, ME 04474

Bart Hauthaway, 640 Boston Post Rd., Weston, MA 02193

Betsie Bay Kayak, Box 1706, Frankfort, MI 49635

Cal-Tek Engineering, 36 Riverside Dr., Kingston, MA 02364

Camp Lake Kayak & Canoe Co., 88 Princess Margaret Blvd., Islington, Ontario, Canada M9P 2Y9

Current Designs, 10124-G MacDonald Park Rd., Sydney, BC, Canada V8L 3X9

Destiny Kayak Co., 1111 S. Pine St., Tacoma, WA 98405

Dirigo Boatworks, Ltd., 616 S. Wichita, Wichita, KS 67202

Dragonworks Inc., RFD 1, Box 1186, Bowdoinham, ME 04008

Dunn's Custom Built Kayaks, 8991 Gowanda State Rd., Eden, NY 14057

Easy Rider Canoe & Kayak Co., Box 88108, Seattle, Wa 98138

Eddyline Kayak Works, Paine Field South, Bldg. 302, Everett, WA 98204

Feathercraft, 1244 Cartwright St., Granville Island, Vancouver, BC, Canada V6H 3R8

Folbot, Inc., Box 70877, Charleston, SC 29415

Georgian Bay Kayak, Ltd., S. S. 1, Site 7, Comp 19, Penetanguishene, Ontario, Canada L0K 1P0

Gillies Canoes & Kayaks, Margaretville, Nova Scotia, Canada B0S 1N0

Great River Outfitters, 3721 Shallow Brook, Bloomfield Hills, MI 48032

Hydra Kayaks, 5061 S. National Dr., Knoxville, TN 37914

Klepper America, 35 Union Square West, New York, NY 10003

Loon Kayaks, Box 253, Smallpoint Rd., Sebasco Estates, ME 04565

Mariner Kayaks, Inc., 127 Lake St. South, Kirkland, WA 98033

Morley Cedar Canoes, Box 147, Swan Lake, MT 59911

Nautiraid USA, Box 1305, Suite 238, Brunswick, ME 04011

Necky Kayaks, Ltd., 1100 Riverside Rd., Abbotsford, BC, Canada V2S 4N2

Northstar Kayak & Canoe Co., 40 Ayer Rd., Locust Valley, NY 11560

Northwest Kayaks, 15145 NE 90th, Redmond, WA 98052

Pacific Canoe Base, 2155 Dowler Pl., Victoria, BC, Canada V8T 4H2

Pacific Water Sports, 16205 Pacific Highway S., Seattle, WA 98188

Paluski Boats, Box 147, Grand Island, NY 14072

Pygmy Kayak Co., Box 1529, Port Townsend, WA 98368

Rainforest Designs, Ltd., 26031 102 Ave., Maple Ridge, BC, Canada V2X 8X7

Rockwood Outfitters, Ltd., 699 Speedvale Ave. W., Guelph, Ontario, Canada N1K 1E6

Seavivor, 576 Arlington Ave., Des Plaines, IL 60616

Seda Products, Box 997, Chula Vista, CA 92012

Southern Exposure Sea Kayaks, Box 4530, Tequesta, FL 33469

Superior Kayaks, 213A Dartmouth Ct., Bloomingdale, IL 60108

We-no-nah Canoe, Inc., Box 247, Winona, MN 55987

APPENDIX

West Side Boat Shop, 7661 Tonawanda Creek Rd., Lockport, NY 14094

Wilderness Systems, 241 Woodbine St., High Point, NC 27260

Wind Horse Marine, 91 Library Rd., S. Britain, CT 06487

Woodstrip Watercraft Co., Box 1140, Lansdale, PA 19446

Clubs and Organizations

For more, and updated, information contact: Trade Association of Sea Kayaking (TASK), Box 84144, Seattle, WA 98124, (206) 621-1018.

Association of North Atlantic Kayakers, 34 East Queens Way, Hampton, VA 23669

Baidarka Historical Society, Box 5454, Bellingham, WA 98227

Boston Sea Kayak Club, 14 Phoebe Ave., Lowell, MA 01854

California Kayak Friends, Suite A 199, 14252 Culver Dr., Irvine, CA 92714

Cape Kayak Club, Box 2664, Hyannis, MA 02601

Chesapeake Association of Sea Kayakers, 3 Markham Dr., Hampton, VA 23669

Coastal Georgia Paddling Club, 9127 Ferguson Ave., Savannah, GA 31406

Coast Busters, Box 22723, Carmel, CA 93922

Coconut Kayakers, Box 3646, Tequesta, FL 33469

Eastern North Carolina Canoe & Kayak Club, 449 Stapleford Rd., New Bern, NC 28560

Environmental Traveling Companions, Ft. Mason Center, Landmark Bldg. C, San Francisco, CA 94123

Florida Sea Kayaking Association, 3095 67th Ave. S., St. Petersburg, FL 33712

Great Lakes Sea Kayaking Association, Box 22082, 45 Overlea Blvd., Toronto, Ontario, Canada M4H 1N9

Great Lakes Sea Kayaking Club, 3721 Shallow Brook, Bloomfield Hills, MI 48013

Hui W'a Kaukahi, c/o N. Olson, 333 Queen St., #710, Honolulu, HI 96813

Juneau Kayak Club, Box 021865, Juneau, AK 99802

Kanaka Ikaika Racing Club, Box 438, Kaneohe, HI 96744

Metropolitan Canoe & Kayak Club, Box 021868, Brooklyn, NY 11202

Nordkapp Owners Club of America, 47 Argyle Ave., West Hartford, CT 06107

North Sound Sea Kayaking Association, Box 1523, Everett, WA 98206

Ocean Kayak Association of British Columbia, Box 1574, Victoria, BC, Canada V8W 2X7

Oregon Ocean Paddling Society, Box 69641, Portland, OR 97201

Puget Sound Paddle Club, Box 22, Puyallup, WA 98371

Rocky Mountain Sea Kayak Club, Box 100643, Denver, CO 80210

Roofrack Yacht Club, Box 192, Westport Point, MA 02791

San Diego Sea Kayakers, 3130 Myrtle Ave., San Diego, CA 92104

San Francisco Bay Area Sea Kayakers, Box 564, El Grenada, CA 94018

Sea Kayak Association of British Columbia, 16064 80th Ave., Surrey, BC, Canada V3S 2I7

Seattle Kayak Club, 1208 N. 42nd St., Seattle, WA 98103

Sebago Canoe Club, Paerdegat Basin, Foot of Ave. N, Brooklyn, NY 11236

Slackwater Yacht Club, B37 Gate 6 Rd., Sausalito, CA 94965

Tantallon International Sea Kayaking Association, 12308 Loch Carron Circle, Fort Washington, MD 20744

Texas Sea Touring Kayak Club, Box 27281, Houston ,TX 77227

University of Minnesota (Duluth) Kayak Club, 108 Kirby Student Center, University of Minnesota (Duluth), 10 University Dr., Duluth, MN 55812

Victoria Sea Kayaker's Network, 752 Victoria Ave., Victoria, BC, Canada V8S 4N3

Washington Kayak Club, Box 24264, Seattle, WA 98124

Whatcom Association of Kayak Enthusiasts, Box 1952, Bellingham, WA 98227